The Constant Sweetness Within

is collection of personal essays, poetry and photographs; it is a multi-layered artistic project that captures my journey and evolution as human on this planet; but more specifically, it explores my journey as a Black woman navigating the intersections of race, gender, politics, marital status and spirituality. It challenges all of us to be vulnerable, to share our stories–those stories that make us human and connect us to others.

The Constant Sweetness Within

reflections on identity,
marriage, motherhood
and feminism

Tamarra Coleman

Photographed by
Preston Lewis Thomas

Cataloging-in-Publication Data is on file at the Library of Congress.
Library of Congress Control Number: 2023911439
ISBN: 979-8-9883404-0-9 (Hardcover)
ISBN: 979-8-9883404-1-6 (ebook)

Published in the United States by Tamarra Coleman
Book design by Preston Lewis Thomas

A special thanks to the many people who have supported me through this journey of evolution and revelation. Thank you to my editor Michel Wing for challenging me to think deeper about my relationships and thus my story. I also want to thank dear friends who provided feedback on early drafts and helped to confirm that I am, indeed, a writer. Thank you Stanley Johnson, Debi Klein, Dr. Tom Dow, Mark Derszinski and Julius Sokenu. Thank you to my three children: Kyle, Evan and Leo, who gave me permission to share aspects of their stories that help to illuminate my own. And, finally, thank you to my parents who have made sacrifices to provide me a life worth living and, most importantly, a life worthy of a story.

Table of Contents

part four: on feminism

part five: mind and body

preface

I was reading my story for the first time in a public space,

when a gentleman in the room kindly responded with "People spend most of their lives keeping their lives private. Why are you telling your secrets?" I realized then, more than any other time before, that I was standing in a room full of people, some I knew and others I did not know, and I was completely naked. I was sharing my fears, my pain, my sorrow, my dreams. I was standing there, as a Black woman, telling a mostly White audience that I didn't feel "Black" enough growing up. I was sharing, as a married woman, that I wanted to be loved unconditionally by a man who wasn't my father. I was proclaiming the power of feminism through my own experiences. I didn't know what these people would think about me. But something inside made me want to share—share my secrets, tell my story.

I have found through the years that my story is not unique. The only difference between me and other people is that I am willing and compelled to speak, to share my secrets, to be vulnerable. I am naked. Being naked is scary. It's scary because everyone now knows I have cellulite. They now see that my breasts sag; I cannot hide behind that push-up bra anymore. They see me "first thing in the morning" without the makeup. It ain't a pretty picture, but it's real. The most profound thing I have learned from working on this project is that people love me for being real—for being them, for being human. I am human, and humanity is beautiful.

Great writers throughout history have penned essays asserting why they write and what writing means to them. I am in no way comparing myself to those writers. I am, however, asserting that writing is very personal, and it has a purpose beyond the entertainment of others. For me, it has been an entrance into myself. These essays express struggle, doubt, self-loathing, fear, anger and resentment.

These are the lies I have allowed to creep into my psyche over the last forty-eight years. I am no longer any of these things. But it is only because of writing that I can now see that. Writing has given me the space to reflect, mourn and feel the pain, thus enabling me to walk through it. As I write in this moment, I see all that I have become from my willingness to explore and express myself—to use my words. My words on the page are the old iterations. The next iteration is unfolding. And, oh, how lovely it is! In a world of relativity, lovely is only lovely in comparison to that which is not. I write to express the loveliness of the new and the struggle of the old trying to find its way.

James Baldwin says that the writer is a "witness." I am a witness to my own experience and my writing is my testimonial. Like all witnesses, I am flawed and biased. I only see what I think I see. I only know what I think I know. I am, therefore, unreliable. My eyesight is affected by my perspective. My beliefs about myself and the world around me are fettered by the lies that have been leasing space in the corners of my mind. Those voices—those liars—have told me that I am a woman, thus inferior. That I am a wife, thus subservient. That I am a mother, thus responsible for who and what my children choose to be and do. The burden of those lies have cost me years, but writing has allowed me to release those lies and find the truth. It allows me to interrogate those voices in my head. It allows me to challenge the belief systems that shape those voices. Writing is a vehicle to project the silent voice.

Baldwin also says the writer's job is "to speak for the

dispossessed." There are many others who share the same story—others who can't or won't tell it. There are others who are dispossessed. I write my story because I believe we are a part of the same story, the same struggle, the same human experience. After reading Dostoevsky, Tolstoy and Dickens, Baldwin concludes, "I am not the first person to suffer this way. It happened to somebody else. If it happened to somebody else, then I can bear it. If it happened to somebody else, then it is true. If it happened to someone else, I am not alone." I write so that I am not alone. Writing allows me to be in good company. Writing allows me to tell the truth.

I write because I can. I have the skill, the desire, and the luxury to write. Not all of us have those things in equal measure. Writing is a privilege that I have. I write because I want my voice to have a place in the world, a place in history. Writing legitimizes my thoughts, my ideas, my ramblings, my human experience. Writing allows me to show up and to be real.

My stories are the backbone of this book. My stories are why I write. My stories are why my life has meaning. They are the essence of who I am and what I am here for. And, for me, it is a journey back to the constant sweetness within. Oh yes. There is a sweet spot, and I want to experience it as often as I can. I can only get there when I am real, when I am feeling the feeling and experiencing the experience. When I pretend those feelings don't exist or ignore them, I am not allowing myself to be me, to be whole, to be human, to be sweet. So, I share my story with you. Read my story. Then go, share yours.

An Introduction or An Essay on Form

In the pages of this book, I have penned a collection of personal essays and poetry. I have also included photography. As a genre of writing, I prefer to express in the essay form. As an English professor for over twenty years, this makes sense to me. The essay is the standard form for academic writing in the Western world. It is how we make our case. It is how we communicate the importance of an issue to an interested audience. In academia, where objectivity is valued, we do this from an objective third-person point of view. We are expected to remove ourselves, our person from our writing and, thus, our analysis, in order to prove that a thing is or is not true, plausible, or at the very least worthy of discussion and inquiry. The personal essay, however, explicitly rejects this idea. It places the first-person subjective voice at the center of inquiry. The "I" is front and center stage. The "I" is valued as a credible point of view with rich experiences from which to draw conclusions and develop analyses. In this book, I draw conclusions and develop analyses based on my experiences in the world as a Black woman, a mother, a wife and a feminist. In *Black Feminist Thought,* Black feminist scholar, Patricia Hill Collins writes:

> *Because elite White men control Western structures of knowledge validation, their interests pervade the themes, paradigms, and epistemologies of traditional scholarship. As a result, U.S. Black women's experiences as well as those of women of African descent transnationally have been*

routinely distorted within or excluded from what counts as knowledge.

The personal has been rejected in academia as a valid voice and perspective, particularly when that voice comes from a Black woman. When I speak of the *academia,* I am speaking of those ideas and ways of being belonging to the university environment. I am speaking of the history and systems that carry the knowledge created every day in our culture. *Epistemology* is the study of knowledge. It asks the question: How do we know what we know? The academy values knowledge gained through objective research—research that is used to generalize and express a universal truth. The Black women's experience is thought not a part of the universal, mostly because it has never been the basis of serious research and study within the academy; thus, it is an insignificant, niché experience expressed by an insignificant part of the U.S. population.

Consequently, Black women have been subjugated to other locations to tell our stories and speak our truths. I have chosen the personal essay. It allows me to make my case and validate my own experiences and ignore the rules of engagement in academic writing. Black women's experiences carry a unique flavor and focus; but like all human experiences, our experiences, in fact, carry a level of universality. My work is the culmination of my lived experiences as a Black female-bodied person and a reflection of my worldview formulated in the mid-nineties when I was introduced to *Black Feminist Thought.* Since then, as evidenced in my collection of personal essays, I have drawn the conclusion that my experiences as a Black woman are both specific and universal. This can be seen clearly in the themes of my work. In her book,

Collins writes:

U.S. Black feminist thought as a specialized thought reflects the distinctive themes of African-American women's experiences. Black feminist thought's core themes of work, family, sexual politics, motherhood, and political activism rely on paradigms that emphasize the importance of intersecting oppressions in shaping the U.S. matrix of domination...Traditionally, the suppression of Black women's ideas within the White-male-controlled social institutions led African-American women to use music, literature, daily conversations, and everyday behavior as important locations for constructing a Black feminist consciousness.

These locations, of course, are outside of the walls of the academy—the gatekeeper of knowledge. So, I do what oppressed peoples have been doing for centuries. I create a space that legitimizes and humanizes me and my proverbial and literal sisters. This space melds written and visual art forms—prose, poetry and photography. While my product is creative, it is also intellectual and political. It is my aim to reach both the intellectual and the everyday. Unlike the academy, Black Feminist Thought is accountable to everyday Black women. To be validated by "ordinary African American women...Black feminist intellectuals must be personal advocates for their material, be accountable for the consequences of their work, have lived or experienced their material in some fashion, and be willing to engage in dialogues about their findings with ordinary everyday people" (Collins). This framework guides my thinking about myself, my experiences and the world around me. There were many moments in the last thirteen years where I was tempted or burdened by the thought of including scholars in my essays to validate my experiences.

I rejected my own thought. I am glad I did. I know my experiences as a woman, a mother, a black body and a feminist are valid—authentic. These experiences are also shared by many others. There are universal truths inherent in the specificity.

The images in this book reflect an important aspect of the Black female experience specifically, and a woman's experience generally—our relationships to our bodies, our skin, our hair. In 2011, when I finally decided to leave my marital home, I knew I wanted to strip off all of the old and begin anew. It took many years to begin to build a new life, but in that next year, I literally stripped off all of my clothes down to the bare, raw and unfiltered mess I was in that moment, and I allowed a photographer to shoot me. I barely had on makeup. At that time, all the makeup I owned could fit in the palm of my hand. My hair was growing out and in that in-between stage. I was self- conscious about my body. I felt unsexy. I felt unwanted. It was hard, but I needed to go to that place. I needed to reveal myself. I needed to find the truth.

The first photoshoot was in Chicago. Five years later, I moved to Southern California. Still writing, I was compelled to let the photographer shoot me again in 2020. I was in a different place, both physically and emotionally. I wanted to go to the desert—a wide open space with infinite possibilities. Initially, my photographer, my friend, thought I was crazy to want a shoot in the desert. We discussed this over some time, and eventually, there was a meeting of the minds. His work became a critical part of my book. His images tell a story. They tell my story. Not every photographer can capture the essence, the soul of another. He did. He captured the essence of who I am in my flat in Chicago and in the Mojave Desert at Joshua Tree National Park.

This book, the essays, poetry and photograpy, captures the essence of my journey as a Black woman. It is both personal and political. It is, inherently, universal because I am, in fact, human.

The
Constant
Sweetness
Within

sweetness

Sweetness is a cool breeze on a summer day
when the sun has been overly hot
and there is no water in sight.
It is also the smell of a baby's neck,
his hands,
his toes...

Sweetness is the feeling you get when you know you're on,

especially doing something you enjoy.

Sweetness is all that is good and pure and real in the world.

Sometimes I am sweet,

but most times,

I am burdened by the everyday worries and troubles.

To look past that and onto the sweet things is the goal,

the key to unlocking

the constant sweetness within.

part one:
on identity

I AM a Black Woman

You are pretty for a black woman...

You are so articulate...

You have good hair...

You sound White...

Are you mixed?

I AM a Black Woman.

If there is a box,

I'd like to check the

Blackity Black Black one.

I AM so Black, you can't see me at night.

You can't see me in the light of day.

Myopia got you fucked up.

.

I AM the Blackest Black Woman in the room.

I've been fucked by Black men and White men,

like the Black Women who came before me.

Some by choice, others... not so much.

.

I AM so Black, when I spit, ink comes out of my mouth

and falls on the page telling the story of my mother, my sisters,

my grandmother and my aunties and girl cousins.

I AM so Black, when I get into the jacuzzi,
it turns into coffee drunk by millions
because they can't get enough of me.

.

They can't get enough of my mocha skin, my style, my
sass, my ingenuity, my strength,
my magic - Black Girl Magic.

I AM so Black, like the color on the color wheel, I
consist of all colors, all things and all possibilities.

I AM articulate because I can talk White, and
I AM fluent in Black English Vernacular.
I AM pretty for a Black Woman and any other Woman.
My hair is good because it grows out of my head.
I AM mixed with all that is and all that ever was.
I AM a Black Woman.

group hair
~circa 2011

In the Black community hair is everything.

Many of us have spent our lives dealing with our hair. Hair has defined us in ways that demarcate us along political lines. Historically, natural hair signified rebellion—rebellion against mainstream notions of beauty (society), rebellion against our mamas ('cause many of us have heard "You ain't goin' out there with that nappy hair, are you?"), and rebellion against ourselves. Processed or unnatural hair (hair that has been tamed and controlled, as not to offend the masses) signified assimilation. Now, before we get all down on the assimilationists, it's important to understand that assimilating has its perks. Straighter, longer and calmer hair has brought us jobs, men, self-confidence, and compliments from our sisters. Besides natural and processed hair, there is a third category: the "Are you mixed?" kind of hair. This hair is more problematic than one might think. In the Black community, mixed hair seems desirable because it's not synonymous with the Black Power fist (or black fist pick, for that matter), and it's not completely straight, either. It allows for free movement within both worlds, as the owner of the mixed hair might deem necessary. However, for many of us who were blessed and cursed with the good hair, this navigation is not easy.

Throughout my childhood, I longed for straight hair. The

straight hair you get after a one-hour date with the hot comb. Or the outcome from the tingling and burning that comes along with chemical relaxers. I wanted to look like and feel like the other girls, my sisters (both metaphorical and literal) and my mother. I was disgusted by the well-meaning...

"You got that good hair."

"Are you mixed?"

"Look at her pretty hair."

"What are you?"

"Are you half White?"

"Hey Red...."

The last one was the worst. This is a common cat-call by Black men referring to light-skinned women and girls who usually had mixed hair. I didn't want to be different. I wanted to be a Black girl. For years, I begged my mother to perm (meaning permanent relaxer) my hair. Every time I saw my sisters getting their hair permed and pressed (a process done with an iron comb heated on the stove), I felt different—not Black enough. Finally, in seventh grade my mother permed my hair. I got to wear the straight styles, get the roller sets and wear my hair down—this is what we call it in the Black community when your hair is freed from braids, pig or ponytails.

I continued to perm my hair regularly until I was twenty-one. It is no coincidence this coincided with my introduction to feminism, activism and the other movements of the 1960s. As a little girl, being Black meant being inside a singular standard or notion of Blackness, but as a young woman, being Black meant something different. I was learning that Blackness was much more complex and multifaceted. As an emerging feminist, I didn't want to be inside anymore. I wanted to be outside. But not outside in the way that I felt as a little girl. I wanted to be outside in a way that challenged inside/outside notions all together. So, I started wearing my hair natural. My natural mixed hair, that is. The well-meaning comments started again, but they were different (or at least I perceived them as different, as an adult). This time my hair was associated with pop culture. First, there was "Freddie." Freddie was the natural, biracial looking, free spirit on *A Different World*, the popular spin off from *The Cosby Show* in the 1980s. Then there was "Scary Spice" of the popular all-girl band the Spice Girls. I didn't completely love this association, but at least she was subversive.

I've been wearing this style off and on for the last fifteen years, pausing for moments in between to wear extremely short boy haircuts as a personal way to assert my feminism, my power. The long, natural, mixed, wild "Freddie" hair carried freedom with it, but somehow it lacked the power of the super short boy cut that conveyed I was two drinks away from a girl-on-girl fling or that my brain operates on overdrive, so don't say shit to me. Whatever message was conveyed, all attention from the opposite sex shut down when I was in my butch phase. I think I secretly wanted this. I wanted attention not because of my hair, but because I was smart, funny, witty, and talented—I wanted people to notice me, not my hair.

It was one of those pauses in my life when I wanted to feel powerful. I had been thinking about locking my hair. I wanted...I needed something that made me feel strong and confident. So, I went to a local hair salon, seeking a solution to the feeling of powerlessness that permeated my body. I sat down for a consultation with the lead stylist in the salon (also the owner) and I said:

"I want to cut off all of my hair. I can't deal with it anymore. I want something easy. I've got three kids and a full-time job. I can't be bothered with my hair all morning."

Then I looked at her. She had a cute, short jazzy cut, and she had mixed hair to boot.

"Something like your hair," I said. "Yeah, something like that would be good!" She turned to me and looked me straight in my eyes.

"Oh no, this isn't going to work for you, honey. Your hair texture is different from mine. You have a tighter curl. It won't look like this. You have to do what is right for your hair. Don't cut off all of your hair. That's unnecessary. You should get a relaxer. It will make your hair easier to manage and you won't be looking crazy. You'll look nice. My hair always looks nice, because I know what my hair can do."

I am rarely intimidated by people. But, for some reason, this woman scared me. I recoiled. She was around my mother's age and had been "doin' hair" for the last thirty years. And, like many of the Black women of my mother's generation, she talked with confidence in a matter-of-fact kind of way that made me believe her, even though I had spent the last few years working with a national organization on a campaign for safe cosmetics—of which, relaxers are not—and I had committed to not using harmful cosmetics, including relaxers, hair dyes, nail polishes, lotions, deodorants, and makeup. I meekly spit out,

"Well, I don't really like relaxers."

She immediately interrupted,

"Well, I don't know why not? Relaxers have changed since the sixties (I didn't know that we were making comparisons). There are different relaxers for all hair types now. We can put a light relaxer on your hair and you can still wear it natural." Is that an oxymoron?

Before I knew it, I was in a chair with a smock wrapped around me, and the shampoo girl was smearing gobs of chemical relaxer onto my head. It wasn't long until the tingling began on my scalp and then the stinging. Once the chemicals were rinsed out and my hair was washed, I was set down in the stylist's chair where she blew out all semblance of curl the relaxer may have forgotten. She then tamed it even more with the Marcel curling iron. As women in the salon began to surround me, all I heard was,

"Her hair is beautiful."

"She's got long and pretty hair."

When the stylist was done, she turned me around to face the mirror, and it took everything in me to respond to "It's pretty. You like it?" I was only able to muster up a half smile and feeble, "It's nice." I then walked out into the sunlight, and a mild breeze blew my newfound locks, reminiscent of Christie, the Black Barbie doll Mattel debuted in 1968. I sat in my car trying to piece together what had just happened. I couldn't comprehend it. I didn't want a perm! And worse still, I was scheduled to attend the National Women's Studies Association Conference the following week, with Angela Davis as the keynote speaker. How could I hold my permed head up in front of Angela, who fought all those years for Blackness in its natural state?

I've spent the last two years thinking and talking about this experience. I shared this story with a dear friend who cleverly suggested I was "group haired." I asked him what he meant, and he likened my experience to that sociological concept of "group think," when people in a given community or society conform to the thinking of the larger group.

Essentially, they lose themselves.

I lost myself that day.

A month later, I cut off all of my hair.

for those of us
who dared
~circa 2011

On September 14, 1970, Governor of California Ronald Reagan

said this of forced bussing as a way to solve the problem of segregation in a southern California school district:

It is a ridiculous waste of time and public money and will undermine all efforts to improve the quality of our public schools... Forced bussing would also deprive them [the children who would be bussed] of the natural environment of the neighborhood school.

Governor Ronald Reagan didn't live in my neighborhood. Governor Ronald Reagan didn't live in any neighborhood. He lived in the fictitious world of the Hollywood screen where the notion of Manifest Destiny was glamorized. He lived in a world where White men were heroes and the indigenous people of this land were savages who needed to be herded up and put in their proper place, a reservation. Maybe this is what Governor Reagan was suggesting, that I and others like me stay on our reservations, in the natural environment of our neighborhoods. Well, we didn't, Governor Reagan. And, for the record, a ghetto is not a natural environment. A ghetto is a place that is carefully crafted and created by those unwilling to look a sad and vicious history in the face. A ghetto is like that brother with a substance abuse problem in a family of overachievers, that brother who can't keep a job and who has been in and out of trouble his whole life. The rest of the family pretends he doesn't exist and hopes he doesn't show up at inopportune times to embarrass them in front of their overachieving friends. But he does show up, just like the ghetto. It shows up. It shows up because it too is a part of the family, the American family.

And we can't close our eyes to it as it festers in its natural environment. The ground on which it was built was polluted; so too will be its harvest.

Too bad Governor Reagan didn't understand this. Or maybe he just didn't care. Some of us did care, so we got on that bus—both Black and White. I am a part of the we who got on the bus that drove to the other side of town, the White side of town, but I am not part of the initial we. The Black and White people in 1970 who put their children on buses to be schooled in foreign environments were the heroes. Not heroes because they did something dangerous or risky or put their children in harm's way, but because they dared. They dared to do something that was right. I got on the bus in September of 1980. Ten years after a judicial order forced the Pasadena Unified School District to use bussing as a means to integrate public schools. I was not an activist and neither were my parents. I was a beneficiary of this valiant effort by socially conscious people, activists, nervous parents and community members who had the nerve to deal with America's estranged brother. I was in the first grade.

I was a bright child. I read and wrote early, and I loved school. I really did. Something about the classroom has always intrigued me. Maybe that's why I chose teaching as a profession. When I talk to people today about my childhood experiences, they are amazed at how much I remember and how much I enjoyed it—the colors, the bright rooms, the images on the walls, the Discovery Room, the library with those headsets. I loved library time. I loved the field trips to the symphony, the opera, and KidSpace. What I really loved was the learning, the information. School provided a constant flow of new information. Not just information about people in textbooks. I learned about real people, real families, real children who sat next to me and became my friends. I rode the bus for forty-five minutes to go to school in the White neighborhood. Many of those kids were bussed to school in my neighborhood, the Black neighborhood; now it's predominantly Latino. Some administrator somewhere figured out how many students from each neighborhood needed to be bussed in order to create fully integrated educational environments. I loved this arrangement. There is no way my group of lifelong friends would have its ethnic makeup if I weren't bussed. In my core group of girlfriends who I still connect with—we've been in each other's weddings, celebrated childbirth together and vacationed together—there's a Jewish girl, a Filipino girl, and a Scandinavian girl. And, of course, there's me. I knew what ebelskivers were long before the late-night infomercials made the pan popular. This was the result of forced bussing: the United Nations. Besides being exposed to different cultures, I was exposed to a world where higher education was the norm. It was expected. My friend's parents, on the other side of town, were school principals, attorneys, authors and hardworking college-educated immigrants who expected their children to go to college.

This brings me to my parents and my community. I am the youngest of five children, and I am the only child with a college education. In my community, even in my family, higher education was not expected. It wasn't frowned upon, but it wasn't expected. I didn't come from a legacy of formally educated people. And I have come to believe from my own experience and having taught in community colleges for the past twelve years, that it is a challenge, a real uphill battle, to be successful in the academic world without that legacy and without that support, not from just your family, but from your community, your people.

My interest in higher education came from my exposure to a different world. We called it the White side of town simply because most of the people weren't Black. But there certainly wasn't this monolith of Whiteness. There was a great deal of diversity in this non-Blackness. I remember going to a birthday party for a little Japanese boy in my class. His mother brought Japanese candy and dried seaweed for all of the kids to eat. I went to prom my junior year in high school with an Iranian boy whose family was exiled during the Revolution in the late 1970s. I ate Persian ice cream at his house, rose ice cream. My homecoming date was Latino; he drove a convertible Volkswagen Rabbit. And I had a crush on an Armenian boy. He played water polo. I loved the water polo boys.

This other side of town was rich with diversity, but as a kid all I knew is that it wasn't Black. So that was White. On the other side of town, I saw education as a core value. The kids on this side of town were expected to go to college. Not only that, studying hard and excelling in academics was cool. I secretly wanted to be a nerd. In my community being smart wasn't cool. I wanted to be cool, and I wanted to fit in. I spent much of my childhood navigating both worlds. Rather successfully, I'd say. But, for the most part, I kept the two worlds separate. I had my Black friends, and I had my other friends. There wasn't any animosity between the groups, but for some reason they never really came together. I never really came together.

I never really came together because I saw that people in the world beyond my childhood experience lived in separate neighborhoods. People tended to live in communities with people who looked like them, talked like them, and thought like them. They still do. I have lived my adult life attempting to emulate my childhood experience, but my efforts never seem to measure up. I consciously place my children in environments that expose them to children of other cultures, other socioeconomic backgrounds, other ethnicities. I scrape up all of the extra pennies I have so that my children can learn to ski, go camping, get involved in theater groups, have lots of books on their shelves, learn to play the drums, draw, paint, take ballet, go to the theater, and eat sushi, organic chicken, real maple syrup, quinoa and lamb. At two years old, my daughter loved guacamole and falafels. She could say guacamole with a Spanish accent. I take them to a Universalist Unitarian church so they understand religious diversity and respect the ideas of others. We talk about sexual orientation and gender, so they are clear these are complex issues which cannot be placed neatly into the preferred male/

female binaries. This is my way of exposing my children to nature, to art, to humanity.

I work at providing my children a rich and diverse childhood experience. As a kid, I didn't have to work at opening my mind; I was forced to open my mind. And, I am a better person for it. I disagree with the late former President of the United States, Ronald Reagan. If a natural environment is one in which we stay in our homogeneous neighborhoods and hold onto to our narrow-minded thoughts, then this is the time humans need to subvert nature. There are times when it is in our best interests to force people to do the right thing, damn it.

sorrow

Sorrow is inevitable.

At some point in our lives we will all feel sorrow.

It is the bane of humankind.

Our lives are destined to pain and heartbreak.

It can be good, I suppose.

But mostly painful and truly personal.

For no one can feel our pain or sorrow.

I feel it often for the world I live in.

Sorrow for humankind, that is.

What can we do?

How can I make it better?

Be sweeter, maybe.

Be gentler to each other and to ourselves.

Sorrow can hurt, but it can also heal.

on shaky ground
~circa 2012

I was leaving the mall after a day of shopping, a little retail therapy.

As I walked toward the exit doors, I noticed it was raining, raining pretty hard. While others stood and waited patiently for it to stop, I hurried out into the parking lot and ran to my car. The rain was heavy, but who hasn't driven in heavy rain? This was typical of late spring in Chicago. As I began to pull out of the mall parking lot, I realized this rain was heavier than a "heavy rain." Nonetheless, I continued driving, thinking I could make my way through and get home as soon as possible. It got darker and the rain got heavier and the wind began to pick up. Nervously, I continued driving in the direction of my house. I looked around me and saw other cars slowing down, some pulling over to the side. I saw a police car waiting in an empty parking lot. I considered pulling into the lot next to the police car because somehow the idea of a police officer gave me a bit of security, but I reconsidered. I continued to drive, slowly and somewhat aimlessly at this point. I wanted to get home, but the antagonizing rain, a storm really, was persistent in discouraging me from my goal.

I turned off the main thoroughfare thinking I would get a break from the rain on a side street. I have no idea why I thought this—completely illogical. This street was even worse. It was a long wide street that looked endless. The strength of the wind was much more apparent on this road. The force of the rain and the clouds made it impossible to see more than a few feet before me, and large tree limbs flew through the air. I stopped several times trying to think of what I should do. I need to get out of this car and get into a house, any house. I looked at the homes that lined the street, wondering if the people inside would let me in. All of the homes looked void, vacant, like there was no one there or at least no one who wanted to help me. I don't know what I expected to see as I looked at the homes. A Good Samaritan waving me in and out of the rain? Was I delusional? It felt like *The Twilight Zone.* Suddenly, I felt completely lost and alone. My imagination began to overtake me, and all I could see was a tornado lifting up the car and reeling me across the sky. The darkness and the debris flying by made me feel like Dorothy in *The Wizard of Oz.* I even imagined the little white shack flying by. I broke down; I completely fell apart; I lost it. I felt completely helpless and alone. No one was going to get out of their car and save me, and no one was coming out of their house to drag me in and out of the rain. I was going to die, and there wasn't a damn thing I could do about it. I was powerless.

***

The Whittier Earthquake struck in 1987. It was the first earthquake I had ever experienced; I was in eighth grade. At around seven in the morning, I stopped at my best friend's house to pick her up on my walk to school and, as usual, she was running late. My girlfriend, her mother and I were chatting as they got ready for the day. My friend's mother stood in her underwear and my friend was curling her hair when the building moved in one jolt. Then another harder jolt, lasting a few seconds, shook the apartment. My best friend's mother rushed us all under the doorway of the bathroom—this is one of those things you learn living in California. Apparently, the doorway is the strongest structure of a building. We stood there until all the shaking stopped. Then she explained to us it was an earthquake. Growing up in California with earthquake drills at school where the children are directed to get under their desks, one would think I would have been prepared for this. I was not. I was petrified. Seemingly, I was the only one feeling this way. While startled, the two of them continued to get dressed, and my friend and I were hurried out of the apartment to get to school. I couldn't help but think: Would it come again? How hard will it hit the next time? How will I know when it is coming? What if I am under a bridge or something? I didn't have the answers, and neither did anyone else. I was going to die in an earthquake, and there wasn't a damn thing I could do about it. I was powerless.

***

After the Whittier quake, there was the Sierra Madre quake in 1991 and then the Northridge quake in 1994, and a number of smaller quakes here and there and in between—the Landers and the Oakland (the one that collapsed the bridge in San Francisco and interrupted the World series)—all of which have had a major impact on the way I move through the world. I am cautious and aware. I drive quickly through tunnels and avoid bridges and parking structures when I can. I've mapped out all major fault lines in California and the Midwest. I studied geology to gain some understanding of the earth's movement—plate tectonics—and the implications of this movement on my life. I rarely sleep naked.

As I look back to eighth grade, I realize that while the earthquakes certainly shook me up, I was really afraid of being out of control. I moved to the Midwest thinking I could run away from earthquakes, but I was met with the threat of tornadoes. No matter where I am located geographically, there will always be something I cannot control, an area of my life that is left to chance or what some might call destiny or fate. I don't know if I buy these concepts completely. I am an Atheist on most days, a Pagan during the Holiday season. For the most part, I believe our lives are largely directed by our own stubborn human efforts and talents. I am beginning to believe, however, there is a small aspect of our lives we have no control of... and we just hope for the best.

a dialogue with the people before I run for
POTUS
~circa 2012

They named me "Brandy."

They named me because I couldn't come up with a name for myself. I had to have a name, a name that was not my own, a name that I could use to pretend when I was there.

It could have been the light caramel color of my skin. It could have been the brown in my eyes. Or maybe it was because I was the only brandy-colored girl there. Whatever it was, he chose me. He chose Brandy. He was my first and only client. I escorted him to a private room. I escorted him to a place where he could get to know Brandy—the dream, the ideal, the fantasy. Not me. I was much too real. I came with far too much baggage. But Brandy, she was young; she was beautiful; she had a job. She had an important job. We pay a high price for pleasure.

In that room, Brandy danced. Brandy smiled. Brandy seduced. But I remained silent. I pushed down all of the pain, the embarrassment, the shame. I even held back the tears, at least for a little while. I listened to the music. I let it lead me. I imagined I was somewhere else. I swayed my body. I unbuttoned my shirt. I pretended I wanted him. I gave him what I owed him. What he paid for. I needed the money. Then the music stopped, and I ran. I ran to my car, and I cried. I drove off, and I never went back. But Brandy has been with me ever since. Brandy is the part of me that shows up when I can't. I couldn't show up then because she wasn't who I was. But is that who any of us are? It was work. It's all work. I don't judge anymore.

***

I remember the fishing trips we went on. He loved fish. He taught me how to love fish. I learned how to eat fish and spit out the bones. He loved catfish the most. I loved catfish. I loved any fish, really, that tasted like fish. I wasn't afraid of the slime. I held the fish in my hands. I scraped off the scales. I ate the heads. When deep fried, the head was crunchy, and the eyeballs, too. He was from the South, the Deep South, Clarksdale, Mississippi. He migrated North during the Great Migration of the '40s and '50s. They ate everything in the South: catfish, squirrel, opossum, rabbit, raccoon, whatever they could catch. And he could catch anything. He wanted us to eat the rabbit, but we wouldn't eat the rabbit. The rabbit was a pet, not dinner. He sat at that table in that little raggedy kitchen by himself. He ate the rabbit. There were chickens, a rooster, dogs and a turtle. That's all I can remember. He had a Doberman Pinscher and a Saint Bernard, Luke and Duke. They were always fighting in the yard, in the back of the truck, in other folks' houses. He took those dogs everywhere. They used to jump out of the back of the truck on the freeway. He had to pull over and catch them before they got run over. He drove raggedy trucks and even worse cars. He used to start the trucks with a screwdriver. The ignitions were broken. Even his tractors were raggedy. But he could fix them. He was from the South. He came from a family of sharecroppers, a legacy of slaves. Whole nations were built by men like him. He worked in construction. He owned a backhoe. We used to go to the swap meet on weekends. He'd buy all kinds of junk. We got skates. We loved to skate. All the kids in the neighborhood loved to skate. We'd make a train. We held on to one another and went cruising down the hills. He bought a go-kart, too. The kids would take turns getting rides down the block. Then we'd jump off the go-kart and onto the tire swing. That was fun. He had an avocado tree, a tangerine tree, too. The dogs used to pee all over the tree. Maybe that was why the fruit was so sweet. I used to ride with him in the front seat of the truck on the freeway, and I would read the highway signs. He loved for me to read the signs. He was impressed by my words. I later learned he couldn't read. He was illiterate for most of his life. But he could start that car with no ignition. He could build a house. He could catch a fish, a squirrel, an opossum, and a rabbit too.

I used to sit in the boat with him when we went fishing. It was an old aluminum boat, a raggedy boat. The motor would stop running in the middle of the lake, or pond, or sea. It was the Salton

Sea. I think it's gone now. All dried up. Nothing but salt left. I sat in that boat. We sat. He was my grandfather. My grandfather was a pedophile. I don't judge anymore.

***

I was young, immature and unprepared to take care of me, let alone a baby. I was going to a community college at the time. I was trying to get enough credits to transfer to a university. No one else in my family had finished college. Most of them didn't even start. I wanted to finish. I wanted to be educated. I wanted to go somewhere. I didn't know where, but I knew I wanted to go somewhere different. My boyfriend was in college too. He wanted to go somewhere. He was smarter than me, though. I would have carried the pregnancy if he hadn't pushed. The truth is I didn't want a child either. I just wanted him to love me. At nineteen, I would have done anything to get him to love me. Even have a baby. But he didn't want a baby, so I didn't have a baby.

I was thirty-two, married with two kids, living in a big new house. I had a Master's degree and good health insurance. What more could a woman ask for? After working three years in a tenure-track teaching position for a community college in Chicago, I had just accepted a fellowship doing policy work at a non-profit organization working on reproductive justice. I had a lot going on. I had a lot of options. I was finally doing some of the things I wanted to do. I was finally becoming me again. Ironically, I found myself at a reproductive rights conference several weeks pregnant, when I didn't want to be pregnant. I remember an older sister in the Movement saying that she couldn't understand how so many young sisters in the Movement find themselves with unwanted or unplanned pregnancies, especially since they work educating other women about family planning and contraceptives. I had birth control at my fingertips. There was no excuse for me having an unwanted pregnancy. The excuse I did have, most women, particularly feminists, couldn't understand. Of course, a major tenet of feminism is that women should have control of their reproduction. And, many women do, thanks to the work of the women in the first, second, and now the third wave of the Feminist Movement. But for me it wasn't just about having control as an independent entity; it was about my husband understanding the responsibility he shared in our relationship.

Consequently, I found myself pregnant. He didn't see birth control as his responsibility. Despite the fact I had birthed two children and had depended on hormonal contraceptives for many years prior to giving birth, he did not take the position that it might be time to give my body a break and carry some of the burden and stress that comes along with constantly thinking about the possibility of being with child. No, he didn't do that. And, for some silly reason, I believed that willing him to think this way, and continuing to fight for the reproductive rights of marginalized women and girls, would somehow change his mind and prevent an unwanted pregnancy. In the meantime, of course, he still wanted sex, even during those times when I said I was close to ovulation and could possibly get pregnant. And he got it. Because that is what a good wife does.

What I didn't know then is that I was one of the marginalized women. We are all marginalized. We crawl along the margins of his world until we demand a space in the center. Back then, I never demanded a space in the center. I thought the work was enough. I thought my ideology was enough. I was fighting for the cause, but my activism was for them, those other women—the unemployed, uninsured or underinsured, the uneducated, the uninformed and the misinformed. They needed an advocate for their rights. Not me. I was not fighting for me. I should have been fighting for me. I couldn't have a third child at that time. There was a lot of work to be done. I made an appointment and a choice between two evils. I don't judge anymore.

I don't judge anymore because I realize life happens to all of us. No matter our politics or positions. We live in the real world with real world experiences. Our lives don't mirror the talking points. Talking points are just that, talk. No one in our bogus two-party system has a monopoly on morality or family values. All of our lives are, quite frankly, messy. If you want an elected official without flaws and a human history, call God. And if the current state of religious affairs is any indicator, He's a hot-mess too, or She. I am banking on God having a little man in the boat.[1]

---

[1] "LITTLE MAN IN THE BOAT"- SLANG FOR CLITORIS.

part two:
on marriage

the doormat

Patiently it waits

firm with integrity.

It does not move or alter its shape despite constant

trampling.

Taking the shit of others year after year,

finally it crumbles and

is quickly replaced.

why did I get married?
a rant
~circa 2011

They say we are waiting on a Knight in Shining Armor.

I'm just waiting on a man who realizes we are in the 21st century. He doesn't have to be a knight; hell, he doesn't even have to own a horse. He could even be standing in the unemployment line, for all I care, because I got that covered. Sex is not a duty. It certainly isn't my duty. I had a non-traditional wedding with non-traditional vows officiated by a Unitarian Universalist female minister in a pantsuit who agreed to omit all mentions of God in our service. When did it become my duty to provide sex, regardless of where I am in my life and how I feel about it? When did it become en vogue to reprimand a woman with three kids under nine, a full-time career and future aspirations for "fucking like a corpse"? Hell, I am a corpse. I am the walking dead. I am dead to myself. My life belongs to others. My values are dictated by others. My responsibilities are for others. Other people. Other incapable, and God knows, capable people.

What more should I be doing? Should I inject Botox into my labia to tighten up the parts that childbearing left loose and open? Should I insert a dozen Eveready batteries in my spine to ensure I am in the proper position when needed? Should I take the kitchen twine I've learned to use so elegantly on holiday meats to impress the in-laws and sew my lips together to make sure I "shut the fuck up," as many of us Black women have not learned to do?

What should I do? What the hell do you want me to do? Tell me...I need clarity...I need some direction...some directive... because I can't see where I misstepped. I have already compromised who I am by getting married in the first place. The purpose of marriage is social control, and I reject religion for that reason. I don't need to be controlled. I don't want to be controlled. I don't need a father. I have one, thank you. I have opted to keep his last name. Why not? You expect me to throw out my name and take on the name of a man who is willing to sell me out when he gets a case of blue balls? Screw you, for thinking so lowly of me. It is a man's birthright before marriage to get all of the pussy he could ever store in a deep-freezer in the garage. Isn't it obvious? We all expect a man to have a stripper at his bachelor party. Even a last fling before the old ball-in-chain is mostly acceptable. He gets stripes on his shirt for having slayed, conquered or hit lots of women. Men are supposed to be sexual. On the contrary, if it gets out that we own a vibrator, our value is lessened. Some men won't even allow their women to use them. I can see why. A two-inch vibrator will out-perform any man on this planet and most others. Now we're beginning to see where the problem is.

Men know why they get married.

Women don't.

the essence of a man
~circa 2013

I have always been a social person.

I've always had many friends. By friends, I mean girlfriends. I was the slumber party queen growing up. A sleepover of less than eight pre-pubescent girls was rare. We would scream, shout, and tell stories until the sun came up. It didn't help that my parents were very social, for they condoned this early female bonding. To this day, the most important people in my life are my girlfriends. Without them, I would be lost. I need my girlfriends. They mirror back to me who I am. I see myself in every woman. No matter her politics. She is me. I am her.

After being married for ten years, I yearned for those times spent with just women, my girls. There were times before giving birth to my daughter that I would settle for anyone, as long as she had a vagina. Living in a house with two boys, a husband, and a few times a year, a teenage stepson, was ridiculous. Males are ridiculous. I don't understand them. I don't get missing that big ass hole and peeing around the toilet seat. I don't get the obsession with flatulence. I certainly don't get scatological humor. And wrestling. What's the obsession with wrestling? Keep your hands to yourself! I remember one day looking out of my bedroom window into the backyard and seeing my three-year-old, my six-year-old, my sixteen-year-old stepson and my husband all piled on top of each other, with the youngest on the bottom. All I could hear was "Man up!" I was thinking to myself, "WTF? He's crying on the bottom because there are 250 pounds of human flesh on top of him. And he is not a man; he is three." What was the grown-up in that situation thinking? Oy vey! Yes, my alter-ego is a middle-aged Jewish woman.

There are clear differences between males and females, at least on the surface. But what I've come to realize over the years is that beyond the surface stuff, there is a certain essence that encompasses a man, any man: gay man, straight man, rich man or poor man. And I love it. I need it. I don't know if it is God given or socially constructed, but a slumber party and a weekend in Vegas with a group of women will not do it. I need a man in my life in some capacity. I think it's the yin and yang thing, the masculine and the feminine. There is just something about a man that is wholly delicious. It is not about sex. I don't want his penis; he can keep that to himself; I have my own genitalia. Actually, I'd prefer it if he were a eunuch. It's something else. It's the depth behind his eyes. It's the seriousness of his presence that commands my attention. I trust him. I believe him. I want to open up completely to him. And I do. I know he'll catch me when I fall. And I will. I have fallen. And he was there.

At this point in my life, I am looking for real relationships—relationships that allow for free and full expression of self, relationships that value all parties involved—relationships that are bi-directional. There is give and take. There is self-disclosure. The truth is I want to feel totally, completely, and whole-heartedly understood. I want a deep, rich relationship with a man that is not about sex. There is something comforting and complementing about a male presence. Beyond being male, however, he's got to be intelligent, witty, good-humored, attractive, kind, thoughtful, organized, and attentive. He's got to be a real person, with real emotions. I guess he can't be a man. A man is not a real person. It's an archetype, a role. A man is bound by societal and cultural expectations. A person, however, is free to be who he wants to be. I've seen this man before. I know him well. He has been in my life for two years. I see him once a week, every week for fifty minutes. I am glad I have a PPO.

faith

Shedding all notions of impossible,

holding truth within the mind of constant ramblings,

running toward that which is

farthest from the present,

knowing it will soon occupy the present space.

the christmas wish of
a middle-aged
black woman
~circa 2021

Dear Santa,
This Christmas, I want a man.

I don't need a man. I want a man. Santa, I don't want any kind of man. I want the kind of man who knows it is far greater to be wanted than to be needed. I want a man who is gentle enough to run his fingers over the soft curves of my body, yet strong enough to not flinch when he reaches the jagged edges—there are jagged edges, and they cut. They cut deep. Those edges have a history; I have a history. I am no blank slate.

I want a man whose interest is piqued by my history, my story, my losses, my gains. I want a man who knows that my history and my hard edges make my soft curves sweet. I want a man who understands you cannot have one without the other. I want a man who can see beyond my brown eyes and full breasts and deep into my soul. Santa, I want a man who will allow me to cry and completely fall apart in his arms and lay close beside him just underneath his armpit to inhale the faint musk that only a man can emit. I want to be intoxicated by his essence. But I want this man to reciprocate. I want him to gift me with his tears, his pain, and his deepest pleasures. I want a man who loves my vulnerability and my strength. I want a man who leaves his ego at the door and embraces his full humanity and mine. I want a man who is not afraid to fail, a man who is contemplative, a man who lives life in shades of gray.

I want a man who sees sex not as an end, but as the beginning of a deeper connection that merges the body with the spirit in a way that he feels my pleasure as intensely as he feels his own. A man who sees my body equally as a place of pleasure and a place of refuge but never a place that he owns. I want a man seasoned enough to appreciate the life lived on the surface of my body. Every scar, dimple, crease and gray hair deserves his respect, reverence even. I want a man who understands when he enters into my sacred space, he owes me nothing, yet everything. Everything is wrapped up in respect. I want a man who knows when I shed the artifice and allow him to see my bare body, my nakedness, I have granted him access to a part of me that is inextricably connected to my spirit, and that spirit reaches the depth of my soul—the part of me that yearns for a deep connection beyond the body...I want a man who understands this does not mean I seek marriage. Marriage is a social construct. What I seek is love. Marriage is a contract made by man that can be dissolved at any time. Love is an agreement between souls. Love is a deep respect for another—another's strengths, weaknesses, desires, freedom, growth and purpose. I want a man who truly loves women. Not just women's bodies, but their souls, their spirits—the essence of a woman.

The serious look on my face—some call it angry—is not because I haven't loved; quite the contrary. I know love very well. I have loved deeply. My love runs as deep as the Atlantic where my ancestors are buried. But in that love, I have met pain—love's first cousin. That pain has left me weary, weary of giving my heart and soul to another. That is how I love, this middle-aged Black woman. I love with my soul. I give all of me—the body and the spirit. I don't know no middle ground. After many years, Santa, I am ready to love again. I have filled up many cups. Now I want my cup filled. I want the love to runneth over. I want to receive in every way all this man has to offer.

But if you can't find this man, Santa, I don't want a man at all. I'll take the rocking horse.

part three:
on motherhood

confessions of a
bad mom
~circa 2019

I am a bad mom.

I yell a lot.

I yell because I am afraid, mostly.

I am afraid because I want to protect my kids from what I know is
out there, and I cannot. So, I yell.

I yell because my marriage failed, and I could not make it work.

I feel alone. So, I yell.

I yell because I want my children to be all the things
I could not be.

I feel selfish. So, I yell.

I yell because I do not understand my children's generation, and I
yearn so deeply for the days long gone.

I am getting old. So, I yell.

I yell because I am so good at other things,
but parenting... not so much.

I feel like a failure. So, I yell.

I yell because children creep into all of your spaces,
both physically and mentally.

I cannot breathe. So, I yell.

I yell because I have been thinking all day about that chocolate
chip cookie dough ice cream,
and when I get home, it is all gone.

The kids ate it. So, I yell.

I yell because being a mother has exhausted me,

and physical activity is on the back burner.

I feel fat. So, I yell.

I yell because it angers me that our society has a penchant for

secrecy and pretensions,

and no one wants to tell the truth about motherhood.

They smile pretty for the camera.

I feel isolated in my truth. So, I yell.

I yell because I live in a society that values individualism

and the nuclear family.

I want a community, a tribe to support me. So, I yell.

I yell because I am not Superwoman, and

I do not have superpowers.

I feel helpless.

So, I yell.

la regresión[2]
~circa 2022

[2] A SPANISH WORD MEANING A RETURN TO A PREVIOUS; A SETBACK

The snow fell softly outside my window as I packed my three-bedroom flat in Chicago.

It was December 2016. While the excitement of returning home to California after eighteen years was apparent on the surface, something deep within me was questioning my decision. The snow was beautiful. It was gentle and calm. The lights from the Christmas tree flickered, and the blanket of white snow on the ground provided the perfect backdrop. The kids were gone; the flat was quiet. Their father had planned Christmas with his family in Oakland, so he drove our kids in my minivan ahead of me. We were separated; we had been for five years. I only had two weeks. I had been offered a position in an English department at a community college in Southern California. I had to start in January 2017 if I wanted this job, which gave me two weeks to pack up three kids and move. What I really wanted was to go home, so I accepted. In the two weeks I packed, I was alone. I was alone packing, making arrangements, looking for a rental property, preparing for the moving truck, sorting our stuff and deciding what we needed to take and what we needed to let go. It was bittersweet. I had become a part of the city; the city had become a part of me.

My entire adult life was formed in Chicago: my career, my

marriage, my family, my community—everything. The city showed me love as a graduate student on the north side of Chicago and as a mom and college professor on the south side. I learned to love anticipating a break in the weather to enjoy a walk downtown or a stroll along Lake Michigan. I became accustomed to seasons and the transition that comes along with the seasons. My favorite is fall. I named my third child and only daughter Autumn for that very reason. It's the sweet spot on the seasonal calendar. There is a crisp smell and chill in the air, but the sun still shines brightly, and the trees put on a magnificent show. I spent as much time as possible with the kids rolling in the leaves and walking in the neighborhood to our local parks to remark at the colors of the canopies. It is the beginning of the transition into harsh, cold winters. This time of the year in Chicago is cool enough for a sweater and boots without the hassle of a winter coat. I learned to love the winters as much as I loved fall. The changing seasons—the impermanence—taught me about life and change. Going home meant reconnecting with my childhood, my family and my community. It meant I would return to the old, the past. But there was no old. There was no past. Returning home wasn't returning at all. I was entering a new place with new people.

My first year back in California was culture shock. I worked at a predominately White institution. We lived in a predominantly

White neighborhood. We found White doctors and dentists and therapists. The kid's schools had all White teachers and administrators and mostly White students. The police officers were White. We left a city where Black doctors and dentists and insurance agents and principals and police officers and attorneys and therapists were readily available and present. A Black woman aided me in giving birth to all three of my children. She understood what it meant to be a Black woman in the healthcare system. The pediatric dentist for my kids was a Black woman. My dentist was a Black woman. My marriage counselor was a Black man. He understood my cry to find my voice in my marriage and then my deep desire to end it and find autonomy. The assistant principal who suspended my son for fighting was a Black woman who disciplined him with love and empathy. My son's therapist who helped him cope with his ADHD was a Black man. The city was ripe with Black professionals and culture. This new suburban life, not so much. I was alone. I was alone as a parent. I was alone as a Black woman. I was alone as a liberal feminist in a conservative community. This is not what I remembered of home growing up.

A year and a half later, I went back to Chicago for the summer in hopes of finding myself. By that time, my eldest son, Kyle had gotten caught up in drugs in his first year of high school. This was the ritzy high school in Westlake Village, California—not the inner-city high school in the Chicago Public School system. I lost my eldest brother, Keith, that same year to an overdose. He was found on the floor of his apartment unconscious and later died. He was somewhat estranged from our family. I don't know if the drugs killed him or the HIV status he had been living with since the 1990s. But it was all too much. Maybe I made a mistake moving my kids across the country trying to find what once was. Maybe I was a terrible parent for moving away from their father. I felt like I couldn't do the single parent thing. It felt like failure on a grand scale.

After eight weeks in Chicago in my marital home, I decided to return to California. No one at work knew I was considering staying in Chicago and not returning in the fall. I even contacted my former institution, thinking maybe they could hire me back. I left in good standing. I made tenure and was a valued professor. But I couldn't stay. I had to go back. I had to go back to face my past, my childhood. What I realized, after I returned, is there were demons I ran away from when I moved to Chicago in 1998. What I had romanticized as a return to my happy childhood was a return to unfinished business almost twenty years earlier. In that next year, Kyle was admitted to a residential treatment center for sixty days. It was the hardest thing I ever had to do. After watching him miss school, run away from home for days on end, fight with his brother and with me, punch holes in the doors in our apartment, threaten to kill himself, I had to do it. The two-hour drive to the house for troubled teens was excruciating. I knew very little about this facility. What I did know, I learned from their website and a telephone conversation. I left my child in the hands of strangers for two months. I believed and still believe today I had no other choice.

I thought that my son being in rehab was the worst of the experiences I would have as a parent. I was so wrong. A year later in 2020–the beginning of the pandemic—my youngest son, Evan, was hospitalized for five months with a life-threatening autoimmune condition. When I was finally advised to take him to the Children's Hospital Los Angeles Emergency Department, he was close to death. I had no idea. According to the specialists, there was no way for me to know. I responded appropriately. Of course, I felt like a failure. I am his mother. I should have known. During this time, I also lost my second brother, Maurice, in the same way I had lost my first two years earlier. He was found on the floor of his apartment. The toxicology report identified an overdose of cocaine. He was also unhealthy and had recently lost several toes due to diabetes. It was all too much. I was alone through all of this. Covid is partially to blame, but the absence of a community, and people with capacity to support me in the way I needed to be supported was also to blame for my feeling of being alone and isolated and lost. I was home but it was not home. I was living in a nightmare. Tragedy after tragedy struck with no end in sight. Just when I thought I was recovering from one traumatic event, another emerged. Through all of this, my youngest child, Autumn—who struggled with her gender identity in middle school, and preferred to be addressed as Leo—was dealing with serious mental health issues. The isolation created by the pandemic and the lack of attention in the last few years because of our hyper-focus on the boys and their problems, sent her into a depression. In her final year of middle school, she took pills with the hopes of killing herself and was admitted to an adolescent mental health facility on watch for seven days. When she returned home, she was put in a partial home hospitalization program for teens with mental health problems. This lasted a week before she was asked to leave for breaking the rules. She was rebellious. This was a difficult time for her. I didn't think I would make it through this stage, but I did, and she did. Being a mother is hard. Being a single mother is harder. Being alone in your own home with people all around you for six years was the hardest.

I came home looking for something that was long gone. I came home looking for my family. The family I had chosen by marriage didn't work, but the family I was born into didn't work too well either. It took me leaving for almost twenty years to figure that out. My experienced adult eyes saw my family differently. It saddened me. It is obvious we all love each other, and we show up for each other at important moments in life, like childbirth, weddings, funerals, graduations, holidays and financial downturns. But what I needed at this point in my life wasn't tangible. I had a deep longing to connect, to be vulnerable and to be seen. I was hurting. I was afraid. I felt lost. My ideal homecoming was a fantasy. My family couldn't provide that connection because of the walls we built to protect ourselves from the pain in our lives. There is so much pain and history in my family that has not been uncovered. I know it's there. I know because I know pain, and I can see it clearly.

Coming home was not coming home at all. It is simply another stop on my journey. Right now, I am here. I am in California. My heart led me back after eighteen years of growing up and messing up. But it's not home. The home I was looking for in California is in the past. The past is gone. We can't go back. We can only go forward. Right now, I am here until my heart leads me to my next destination.

down boobies
~circa 2013

I was stepping out of the shower, naked, as I usually do,

and my daughter who was almost three at the time was sitting and watching television in my room.

She looked up at my naked body with great pleasure and announced, "Mommy, you have down boobies." Then she looked over at my thirteen-year-old niece who had just walked into the room, and said, "Joie has up boobies." The proverbial bubble began to inflate over my head with a caption that read: "I had up boobies too, before I had you." Of course, with my filter on and fully composed, I replied, "Oh, thank you dear. That's the look I was after." It was that moment which confirmed my contention that children are always watching and always judging. Always judging! Or maybe they are observing and simply stating the facts. Nonetheless, the old saying that children are a blessing from God is a lie. They are from the devil, just like high fructose corn syrup and partially hydrogenated oils. They eat at you. They bug you. They nag at all of your anatomical systems. They wear you down, and they kill you. They suck out all of your energy and they kill your spirit.

Just recently I was planning summer activities for my children, trying to get them involved in the most enriching experiences I could find. My middle son has a strong affinity for music. He took drum lessons and has an amazing sense of rhythm and timing. He had been asking to take guitar lessons—we have an old guitar that his older brother once played and then tossed aside after two or three sessions. So I started looking for a class for him and happened upon a class for parents and their children. This seemed like a great idea given that I have always been interested in learning to play. I imagined us going to class together every Saturday and spending quality time helping each other develop musically. "Wow...that would be awesome," I thought. I presented this idea to him in the form of "Hey Evan, I found guitar lessons that you and I could take together. Wouldn't that be fun?" He responded with a look of disgust and a short "Uh...no." I looked over at my eldest son and asked, "Wouldn't you want to take a guitar class with mommy?" His response was equally as disturbing. Evan, my middle child replied, "I do want to take guitar lessons, but not with you." I was crushed. He's only seven and he is already finding my presence repulsive.

When I was pregnant with my first son, I gained forty-five pounds. After giving birth, I shed only ten of those and held on to the other thirty-five pounds for almost ten years. It was really depressing. As a single woman with no kids, I maintained a lean body between a size four and six. I was fit. I was physically active, and I ate a mostly healthy diet. After having children, I found myself perpetually exhausted, both mentally and physically, which did not promote thinking about a balanced diet and exercise. I hated my postpartum body. My belly maintained the roundness of a six-month-pregnant body for many years. My breasts were so large, I had to buy all new bras and those still didn't fit right. As a younger woman, I went braless most days or wore those bras that are like camis. I didn't need any extra lift or support. The worst part was the fat that lingered in my face. Every time I saw my reflection, I felt pregnant, fat, undesirable. I stopped looking in mirrors and shied away from photographs. It didn't help that my children often commented on my weight. I often heard things like,

"Mommy, is there another baby in your belly?"

"You're chunky, Mommy!"

"Mommy, you're fat!"

And, of course they loved to squeeze my middle section and smile, as if I were a cute little pet pot-bellied pig that they could squeeze and cuddle at their discretion.

Before he went off to college, my stepson would come out to visit with us during the summer. I remember one summer when he was around twelve or thirteen. He overheard me talking about wanting to lose weight and going on a diet. I was sitting at the counter one afternoon, eating a bowl of ice cream or a pastry or some other decadent carb of choice, and he said to me, "You're never going to lose weight if you keep eating that." The look on his face was dead serious. There was not an inkling of sarcasm or maliciousness in his voice. But somehow, his comment felt like a judgment. It was so matter of fact. It was so raw. It hurt. It was the truth. The truth sucks. If you don't want or can't handle the truth, then don't have children.

Being a mother is like being a wife. It's not me they want; it is something from me—buy me this, take me there, help me with this, give me that. It's a duty, a role, and it's thankless. The difference between wifedom and motherhood, however, is that you can cease being a wife, and you never have to travel that road again. With motherhood, it never ends; it's never over; the title is there as long as a mother and her children are alive. Even when they don't like you, they seem to need you. They need you when they need you, not necessarily when you want them to need you. When those times come when they don't need you, it feels like rejection. But, it's not rejection, it's independence; a child needs to find his way. When I have been able to experience the rejection and get past it, I have learned that a mother/child relationship is like any other relationship. Children are independent beings with independent thoughts, ideas, desires, hopes, dreams, likes and dislikes. I have tried, far too often, to project my will onto them. I thought that was what I was supposed to do as a mother—tell them what to do and how to do it. So when they don't want to do or be, I feel like a failure, a failure because they are not exactly who and what I want them to be. They are not exactly, well, me. What else can I give them, but who I am? When who I am isn't enough for them or right for them, what does that say about me? I believe it says I am me and they are them. Even though I carried my children for nine long months within the warmth and comfort of my body, and I birthed them through my womb, I do not own them. I am merely here to help them and to guide them in the direction in which they want to go. I am powerless over the journey of their souls.

Children are not here to bring us joy; they are here to teach us lessons. They teach us lessons about life, love, and sacrifice. They make us real. They show us who we really are. Women often talk about motherhood as the single most important experience in their lives. I am not sure if I agree, but I am not sure I completely disagree either. Motherhood is certainly meaningful and certainly an experience, but I am not sure it is the most important experience in my life. I think of myself as the sum total of all of my experiences. If I had not become a mother, there would be another equally important experience to take its place. In a world where the very few own all of the resources and the rest of us sit by the table and wait for the scraps, I am not sure if bringing more life into the world would be my first choice if I had a do-over. But, being a mother has, certainly, helped me become comfortable with my true self, all of the flaws and imperfections, down boobies and all.

My Hopes for Evan

He feels loved.

He feels valued.

He finds his passion.

He lives life to the fullest.

He laughs more often than not.

He knows success.

He finds love.

He camps under the stars.

He travels around the world.

He learns to use his strengths.

He learns to accept his weaknesses.

He learns to trust others.

He learns to trust himself.

He goes the extra mile.

He dances freely.

He loves deeply.

He eats the street food.

He finds the backroads.

He talks to the stranger.

He sees the soul of another.

He follows his north star.

He shares his gifts with the world...

gratitude, growth,
pain and love
~circa 2023

I cannot empathize.

I don't know what this is like. I am careful to catch myself when I want to say to him 'I know this is hard for you.' No, I don't know anything about what he is thinking and feeling, and I am sorry for that. I cannot take this away from him; I cannot fix this, and that is very difficult for me.

It came back. The inflammation caused by the disease began to manifest physically in his body. The symptoms, now recognizable: conjunctivitis, ear infection and then swelling in the knee and pain in the joints, returned one by one. Out of sight. Out of mind. Despite the regular medical appointments—for check-ins and checkups, infusions and lab samples—it felt like it was over. It felt like remission. The medication was working...wasn't it? The medication was and is working. And the disease is still with us. Both are true. He has to live with granulomatosis with polyangiitis, GPA. By proxy, his mother has to live with it, too. I am his mother. When he wails in the middle of the night with aching joints and shooting pain, I can hear him. The sound of the moans of a boy who is almost a man wake me out of my sleep as easily as when he cried as a baby. The baby could be pacified with milk or swaddling or a gentle touch. I had the power to console my baby. I had some control. He is no longer a baby. His pain and discomfort are more complex. A mother's touch cannot heal him.

It was when the pandemic hit in March 2020 that my middle son Evan fell ill. In the span of ten days, he grew progressively worse—worse being close to death. Initially, we assumed it was Covid 19. After three visits to his pediatrician and several tests, it was recommended that we immediately head to the Emergency Department at Children's Hospital Los Angeles. He lost ten pounds; he could barely walk, and his blood oxygen level was 52. I believe if I had waited any longer to drive to the emergency room, I would have lost Evan. Our journey began on April 8, 2020. It wasn't a linear journey. There were setbacks and highs and lows. It was a time of deep learning for me as a mother, as a woman, and as a human on this planet. I felt powerless and the need to control all at the same time. It took everything in me to leave the hospital for some respite the first week after five straight days of sitting by Evan's side in the intensive care unit.

4/12/2020

I left the hospital yesterday, and Evan's father Ron is with him now. He drove out from Chicago and arrived late Friday night. I will return to the hospital tomorrow. It was very hard to leave because I couldn't help feeling like I was leaving Evan. But, a big part of this journey is learning to trust other people. I have a tremendous level of trust for the work the doctors are doing at Children's Hospital Los Angeles. I am learning to let go. Kyle and Autumn are managing well. I am very proud of Kyle for managing for two days with his younger sister. The support system from our "village" in Thousand Oaks also helped. He is learning at seventeen years old that at some point we all have to step up, step in and be responsible. This is definitely a growth moment for him. It was good to come home and talk and laugh a little with the other kids and think about something other than the hospital. But, as I got into bed last night, the heaviness of the situation returned. Kyle noticed that I was sad, and he brought Evan's teddy bear, the one I bought when he was born, and placed him on the pillow next to me. It seems compassion pours out of us all when most needed. I love my kids.

As if that first visit to the ER and ICU were not enough, just when we thought Evan was moving in the right direction, things took a terrible turn. Three weeks after being home, Evan's symptoms started to return. That same anxious feeling and lump in my chest returned on this most recent flare up and brought back the memories, the fear, the trauma of 2020. I now know what the disease is and how to best treat it, and I still feel a loss of power as his mother. There was a period during his five-month hospital stay when I felt like I was on an emotional roller coaster with each day bringing another steep hill to climb and overcome. That trauma is with me today. I have to consciously bring myself down from that cliff and, literally, breathe.

5/24/20

It has been just over a week since Evan was re-admitted to the Children's Hospital Los Angeles (CHLA). It was very hard to go through almost the same experience as the first hospital stay: Emergency Room, ICU and then the "floor" (which is the hospital floor for patients that require less intensive care). Although we have not gotten to "the floor" yet. Evan is currently in the ICU and intubated. The goal is to extubate him this afternoon. He is showing much progress in breathing on his own. Currently, he is being tested with only the support of the CPAP and seems to be doing well with that level of support. This time around he had to receive dialysis, as he was retaining too much potassium in his body. That process ended last night. His potassium levels are down to a normal level. He is clearing (coughing) out the secretions in his lungs left there by the hemorrhaging.

The week was a long week of ups and downs and scares. The medical team worked tirelessly to find a balance with all of the medications and treatments for different organs and systems while keeping his vitals in check. At several points his blood pressure dropped due to over sedation. It was probably one of the hardest moments for me since this all began. The first time, I stood in utter shock when I was stopped by one of the attending physicians before I entered the room. I had stepped out to take a shower. My biggest fear is that I will leave the room or the hospital to do something, and I will return to a tragedy. This is what our mind does to make us believe we have some control. Like, if I sit here by his bed and watch every moment of the day, then nothing bad will happen. If this experience has taught me nothing else, it has taught me that I have almost no control—I am hanging on to a little bit! LOL. What impressed me was the physician who over-sedated Evan. He came out of the room, walked up to me, looked me in the eyes and said: "It was my fault. I over-sedated him. I am sorry." For those who know me well, you know I appreciate raw, unfiltered honesty over all else. I stood in silence. Then I walked into the family waiting room and sat and cried. Then I wiped my eyes, put on my big girl panties, and I got back in the game. What choice do I have? The team worked to bring his blood pressure back up and stabilized him, but it got real in here. Clearly, he made it through these mishaps, but those moments, which I suspect are common in the practice of medicine, are hard. I kept remembering what Desta always says, "We can do hard things." Yeah, we can, but this shit is hard hard.

The hard moments strengthened me. While I would never wish this on any parent or person, I do believe this experience is a part of my journey and my growth. I am able to see my son much more clearly. He takes in each moment. He rejects anxiety. He sees no need to worry about the next moment. He lives in the present. I tend towards over planning and preparing. He doesn't plan at all. Evan has shown me, in the way that he has dealt with his disease, how to be in the moment. He has taught me in his actions and this experience has taught me in its existence how to appreciate the little things and acknowledge the small wins. I have spent my life focused on the big accomplishments. I have missed opportunities to celebrate the small things, the mundane, those things that are most important in life.

5/26/20

I woke up this morning in my bed, my very comfortable bed, after three nights in what has become my home away from home--a little nook, like a window seat but the size of a twin-sized bed, with a view of Los Angeles. It's not totally uncomfortable. They provide me fresh linen when I want it. There is a curtain I can draw for a little privacy, but they always know, and most importantly, he always knows, mom is back there. Sometimes I hear him ask or I hear them say to him: "Mom? Yes, she is there." I suppose that satisfies him because that usually ends the conversation. Privacy is relative. When I am there, a curtain feels like privacy. But the ICU is never private, and that is good...sometimes.

Before I came home on Monday for a much-needed Memorial Day repose, I experienced, all of us in that room experienced, the irony of the ICU. It is the space between the Emergency Room and "the floor," a space where patients are cared for intensively before they progress to the sixth floor. The ICU is on the third floor, so, literally, progress is moving up. The irony of it all, as a nurse explained trying to comfort me, is in the ICU it is normal to take a step forward and then two steps back. It is frustrating and sometimes difficult to see the progress. While on dialysis over the weekend, there were complications with the dialysis machine. Sunday was the third cycle of dialysis treatment. Again, the machine beeped signaling air in the line. We had become familiar with the beeping sound. Initially, they thought it was a problem with the machine. It was signaling that there was air in the lines and that is not a good thing. But nothing could be found that explained or identified how the air was getting in. It became clear that the main line running through a vein in his groin area was a little sensitive and positional. It seemed to like being in a certain position and unmoved in order to work properly.

On this third attempt, a new machine was brought in and the cycle was started. The beeping around 2 a.m. signaled problems and several nurses came in and looked, talked to each other, began trouble-shooting until finally they decided it was time to engage the attending physician. The physician came in and finally determined there was a tiny hole in the catheter that connected the line, and tiny bits of blood leaked slowly from this tiny hole. They decided they needed to change it out with a new one. All the while, I am there behind the curtain--the only thing separating me from my greatest fears.

My greatest fear, as a mother, is losing a child. Evan's hospitalization was the second event in two years that brought me face to face with the potential death of a child. Kyle's substance abuse and subsequent admission to rehab was the first. The transition from Chicago to California as he entered high school was challenging for him, and he turned to drugs to cope with the anxiety and depression. He spiraled downward, and by his sophomore year he was heavily involved with the wrong crowd, skipping school and running away for days. Each night he was away, I sat with the fear that I would find him dead from an overdose. My mind always flirts with the worst-case scenario. Imagining the worst allows me to have some control over my response. It prepares me. I wasn't prepared for this. None of this.

When these tragedies happened, the only sense I could make of it all was to blame myself. Maybe Evan wouldn't be sick with an autoimmune disease if I had breastfed him. GPA may not have taken over his body if I had been paying closer attention and seen the signs sooner. Kyle would not have fallen into drugs if I had not moved him to California. My kids would be secure in themselves if I had stayed in my marriage with their father and provided them a life of stability. Maybe my expectations are too high. Maybe they are too low. My fear of death is directly connected to my fear of losing control. I should know better. I should have made a better decision. I have the power to prevent these things from happening. But I don't have the power now and I didn't have the power then to prevent any of this. I cannot control life or death. All I can do is my best on any given day.

6/14/20

I am grateful for Evan's progress. This has been a very trying time for so many reasons, but mostly because it is difficult to play nurse and mom to a kid who was doing dangerous tricks on a skateboard only three months ago. I am learning so much about myself and about Evan during this time. As a parent, we often experience the rough side of our kids, but I get to see the smart, polite and respectful young man who his dad and I are raising.

We are constantly told by the hospital staff how much of a pleasure it is to have Evan. He thanks the staff for every little thing. He is also showing compassion for the other kids here in rehab. Most of the kids are younger and in much more difficult medical situations. He is friendly and kind and bumps fists with the little girls with shaved heads. He smiles and holds conversation with the kids and the staff. It is nice to see. It makes me feel good about him, and it also makes me feel good about me. I am doing a good job. That's all we really want as parents--to know we are doing a good job.

Two days before Evan was hospitalized, he said to me in a weak voice as he lay in my bed feverish and tired, "You are a good mom. Don't ever say you're not." Two days later he was in the emergency room being intubated for the first time in an air tight room surrounded by medical professionals in personal protective equipment. It was the beginning of the pandemic and the beginning of our journey. Before they placed the tube in his throat, he looked at me and reached for my hand and said, "It's okay, mom. I'm okay." He was trying to comfort and take care of me. More recently, now eighteen years old, he came into my room and got into my bed and said, "You always take good care of me." Evan notices. He sees me doing my best. Now I have to believe I am doing my best.

6/25/20

I have not been feeling in the mood to write. I have been more in the mood to think, reflect and stare into space and sit in sadness and discomfort and frustration. The heaviness of all that is around me is starting to settle in my core. As a person who responds to danger with action, I have been in constant motion over the last four months—never stopping to really feel the heaviness of this moment, these moments. Evan's underlying condition is serious. There is no cure. It can cause death. This is the reality. On Sunday, while sitting in the healing garden (the only place Evan gets fresh air and sunlight), he said to me: "What if I am not able to walk again?" He stared into the distance. I looked into his eyes. I mustered up the courage that he has given me to say: "Yeah, that's hard and that feels terrible. Let's think about that. What if you are not able to walk again? Do you think there are people who live full lives in a wheelchair?" He nodded his head and said, "Yes." I said, "It would be hard, but there are many people who learn to live with it. The reality is, though, it is more likely that you will walk again. And, it will take time. You are already gaining strength and muscle."

This is Evan's journey. As Evan's mom, this is also my journey. His experience involves managing a lifelong disease. My experience is managing myself watching him on his journey. It is such a passive and powerless position to be in. It is very different from the active position of parent. I cannot parent my way out of this. I cannot give him any answers. No amount of chicken soup can help. I can sit next to him for days on end and watch movies with him, play connect four, do crossword puzzles together, watch him write in his journal, sit with him in the healing garden, and record him taking his first steps in the exoskeleton.

It is hard for a doer, like me, to do this. So, instead of resting, like I should, I take that energy and pour it into work. I realized over the last few days that my work keeps me from feeling powerless and helps me to feel like I matter and I am doing something. But I also realized that the constant motion only gives me the illusion of power. In our culture, we value movement and action. We have not yet embraced the power of simply being. There is power in presence. I have to learn that simply being there with him is enough. I am enough...and, it is okay to rest.

It took me three years to finally rest. From the moment Evan was hospitalized in 2020 until January 2023, I poured myself into my work. I didn't come up for air. I was on a mission. With the pandemic officially declared in March, Evan's diagnosis in April, the murder of George Floyd in May and the tragic death of my brother, Maurice, in July, I felt like I was losing all control of my world. Everything that could emerge in me emotionally—did. A cloud of death was in the air. The activist in me emerged. I was responding to the trauma all around me. My protector, the Strong Black Woman, came to my rescue. She led me through this. She kept me whole. Without her, I would have broken into a million little pieces. When I wasn't in the hospital, I was at home in virtual meetings fighting for radical change in our institutions of higher education. I even held meetings on Zoom from my little nook in Evan's hospital room. He overheard me advocating for racial justice and strategizing for equity. The medical staff even listened in sometimes. I was asked for feedback from one of the physicians working on Diversity, Equity and Inclusion in the hospital's programs, practices and policies. I had to keep moving; I had to stay busy. I couldn't control Evan's disease, but I found power in activating and organizing people to make social change. It was a very difficult time for me, for Evan, for all of us. There was no time to rest. There was work to be done.

9/4/2020

I haven't posted since June 25th. I haven't wanted to write. I have spent a lot of time wondering—wondering why me? Why my life? I have spent a lot of time feeling like I was dealt a shitty hand.

I have been busy playing my violin.

Since June 25th, Evan spent time in rehabilitation gaining his strength for a couple of weeks, then he had a seizure, caused by the medications, and was sent back to floor. There, we also found he had a staph infection that caused terrible blistering in his mouth and on his face and entered into his blood stream. For a couple of weeks, he remained on the floor in bed taking antibiotics and anti-fungals. Infectious disease was concerned it could be a deep lung fungal infection, and they treated him out of caution. It turned out after removing a sample from his lungs that he did not have a fungal infection, and the staph finally cleared. In his condition, with the heavy immunosuppressants he was on to stop the underlying vasculitis, an infection of any kind could be deadly for him. He finally got better, and was cleared to go back into rehab.

Six weeks was the time estimated that he would need in rehab to be able to do basic self-care without assistance. Six more weeks...He was scheduled to discharge on September 4, 2020. He was first admitted to the hospital on April 8, 2020. He came home today---September 4, 2020. Evan spent five months in the hospital.

It has been a long journey for Evan. He has been our strength, our hope, and full of love. The team in the rehab unit loved having

Evan. They were very sad to see him leave.

"He is such a hard worker."

"He is such a great kid."

"He is so polite."

Through it all, he smiled; he said please and thank you; he kept pushing. I kept pushing. We kept pushing because Evan kept pushing through it all. His life will be different. He looks a little different. He knows this. His body is different. His skin is different. His hair is different. His outlook may even be different. But his spirit is the same. He laughs. He plays video games with friends online, and he swears like a teenage boy. He doesn't think I hear him. He looks at his mother, and he wonders if I am ok. He knows I worry. He knows I am afraid. He sees through all of the veneer. He says, "Mom, stop worrying. I am ok. I got it." He does. I don't.

He is home, and he walked up the stairs, several times, today. We have stairs now. He can walk. He walks differently. He will continue outpatient physical and occupational therapy for a while.

He is home. I can hear him now playing online with friends. He is home. He and his sister got into a verbal match today---his first *day home. She ran off crying. He is home. Life will be the same as it was before April 8, 2020, yet it will be so different. I don't know what life will bring Evan. I don't know what life will bring me. But I am going to play this shitty hand I was dealt. I will do it with gratitude because Evan is home. I will look at it as an opportunity for growth. I will feel the pain and move through it, and I will remember to love. Evan is home.*

These memories of 2020 linger and live on in me. Every day I think about my job as a mother. I vacillate between feeling all powerful and powerless. The goal is to find a middle ground and accept what I cannot control and do my best at what I can.

As I move into the seventh cycle of seven years in my life, I am much more reflective and intentional about how I am using the energy that lies in my soul. I am seeking ways to love, love in the face of difficult circumstances. The one lesson, of many, that I have learned in the past seven years is the only way to the light is through love and acceptance.

Evan has grown up and has finished high school. Despite the life-threatening disease that lives in him, he has found ways to be joyful and to remain positive in the face of his life challenges. I will follow his lead. Maybe, the job of a mother is to learn—to learn how to live and to let go of the idea that we are all powerful—and to love.

part four:
on feminism

the cacti

The harshest of conditions, though it lives

A shield of prickly daggers to protect

Where scarcity of water upends most

Its flower blooms most beautifully despite.

feminism is a
trauma response
~circa 2022

Activism is a trauma response.

The first definition of "activate" is to make reactive or more reactive. Activism is a reaction. It is a reaction that comes from a person that has had a painful experience with an issue; we can call this trauma. Our trauma informs the way we react to things, the way we respond—until we know better. I responded by becoming an activist. I am a doer. I am always activated. The most well-known and researched responses to trauma are: fight, flight, freeze and now fawn. While most of us resort to all of these in some form, we tend toward one response more than others. I am a workaholic. I am achievement driven. I am my own greatest critic, constantly telling myself to do more and do better, be more and be better. I am never enough. There is always another place to go and be, an achievement to be made. An activist has a cause, a purpose, a reason to keep going. An activist is always in flight. Our mission is to save the world. The truth is we are really trying to save ourselves—save ourselves from the trauma.

My attraction to feminism was inevitable. Feminism at its core is a response to trauma—a toxic patriarchal society. Women who identify as feminist are standing up and saying no to being left out, ignored, minimized, objectified, patronized, vilified, fetishized, sexualized, purified, and de-humanized. Our lives, as women, under siege by patriarchy, are traumatizing. We learn to live with it; we learn to cope. Most of us succumb to the power of the patriarchy and respond by fawning—people pleasing. Then there are those of us who respond by reacting. We act up and act out. We are in perpetual fight or flight mode. For many of us activists, the public trauma imposed on us by the system of patriarchy is hard, but it's the trauma in our private lives that causes us to react. I am not afraid to act. I have been doing my whole life—mostly because I have had to. I have never felt secure in the hands of another. That is what childhood sexual abuse does. For most of us, the ones who are closest to us who have abused us, abused our trust. We have trust issues, thus, control issues. We need to be in control. We did not have control as children, and as adults, we are looking to feel safe and secure. We fight off any perceived danger. For those of us who become activists, we fight like hell for others. We are empaths. We feel the pain of others because their stories are all too familiar. We carry your secrets and we bring them to the light. If we are honest, we recognize it is not the other who needs saving. We are saving ourselves from the trauma.

From the time I was seven years old until I was fourteen, I endured sexual trauma. Even now, I feel guilty calling it trauma. There wasn't force, or physical pain or violence. I wasn't threatened. It just happened, and it happened again, and again, and again for seven years. It occurs to me, as I write this, thirty-two years later, I am denying the truth. It was force; I was a child. There was pain; it lives on in my nervous system today. It was violent. My boundaries, my body, my space, my humanity was violated; that's violence. I never gave permission. I never said yes. But I never said no, either. I was silent, and in the silence, there is shame.

Childhood sexual trauma leaves us deficient. We move through the world with blurred lines and broken boundaries. We experienced sex too soon without the pleasure and autonomy. Sex then becomes this very confusing place of both shame and desire. As adults, we often become very promiscuous or repressed and frigid. Neither of those extremes allow for a healthy adult sex life and intimate relationships. Intimacy is about trust, and it is difficult to trust when appropriate relationships were not formed in childhood. All of my adult intimate relationships were deficient or inappropriate—sometimes both.

More than any other, I have relied on the flight response. I am a workaholic. It is through work I experience wins. I am good at work. I am good at doing and creating. I am not so good at being. As a child, simply being and existing made me a target of other people's pain. Simply being feels passive. I abhor passivity. I am an activist. Activism is either reactive or proactive. Either way, it involves action.

Being a feminist, for me, means being on constant alert. It's the lens I use most often to see the world. My gender identity has been more of a detriment than my racial category. In some ways, I have transcended my racial category. I have learned to navigate White spaces with language. I have mastered the art of talking white. As the nice Jewish fella I met online said, "You sound Whiter than me." My ex-husband once said to me, "You are the whitest Black girl I've ever met." Transcending race, to some degree, has never been difficult for me. But my gender, my identification as a woman with a vagina, has plagued me my entire life.

My vagina has been a place of both unthinkable pain and incredible power. I learned very early that I have something that men want. But I also understood the power imbalance. I knew that if I wasn't careful my vagina could be taken from me without my permission—again. I knew I was physically the weaker sex. To account for that, I spent my time learning. I focused on being smart. I vowed to never let a man outsmart me. I did not want to be perceived as the weaker sex. This led to the construction of a wall I built around myself. A wall of invincibility. I became the proverbial Strong Black Woman. The Strong Black Woman persona poses many problems for the sexual abuse survivor. A large part of me walks through the world with shame. I want to avert my eyes and put my head down. But the Strong Black Woman part of me silences the shame. Shame is weak. Shame is vulnerable. Shame is penetrable. The wall I have constructed is a wall of silence. I have silenced all that is weak in me. Feminist activism has allowed me to be strong, to appear strong, to feel strong. But it has diminished my humanity: the weakness, vulnerability, and penetrability.

The Strong Black Woman is a persona we create out of necessity. She is an archetype. Our experiences call for protection, and the Strong Black Woman swoops down and protects us from the abuse; it protects us from the trauma—generations of trauma inflicted on our bodies and on our spirits. She protects us when it seems no one else will. She is me. I am The Strong Black Woman. I am a feminist. I am an activist. I am a fighter. In my flawed and unreliable reality, I am alone in the world. My experiences have shaped my beliefs about others. Others are not there when I need them. As a little girl, a wife and a mother, I thought I was alone. I was not. The Strong Black Woman was there. She saved me from myself. She saved me from the trauma. I need her.

The Strong Black Woman is the quintessence of feminism, but the Strong Black Woman lives on the surface and in the moment. Like all trauma responses, she is meant to be temporary. She is the mask. Underneath, I am fragile. Like glass, I am strong, yet breakable. The assumptions made about me as a Black woman are oppressive. They keep me in a box. Strength is my constitution, but so is vulnerability. I need the world to see my vulnerability. I need you to see my vulnerability. I need you to see me as human.

why I am a feminist
~circa 2009

A few years ago, my father and I were having a conversation—a debate, really.

And he said to me in his usual matter-of-fact kind of way, "You're not a feminist anymore, Tammy! You're a wife and a mother." I was put off by his comment, typical of the end of a conversation with my father. But as I have reflected upon it over the last few years, that statement has provided a point for me to challenge my ideas and my beliefs, particularly those on feminism, marriage and motherhood. It has altered my understanding of feminism. Since then, my definition of a feminist has become much more complicated.

My father has always had a way of getting under my skin. I have never been one to mince words or recoil in the face of a challenging argument. English is my first language, and I have always been able to use it to my advantage. Ever since I was a little girl, words came easy for me. It wasn't just the language itself; it was a keen understanding of the ways in which language and words impact our lives, our experiences and our relationships. It is the ultimate form of expression. It allows us to manifest, in the real world, feelings and ideas that exist in a seemingly separate, sometimes lonely place. Language is a malleable creative force that can shape us, write us into history, and tell our stories.

Words became a comforting resource for me after taking my first composition course at Pasadena City College. I remember Dr. Wilson's class like it was yesterday. He introduced me to James Baldwin, Brent Staples, Angela Davis and Shirley Chisolm. Before this course, no one had ever told me a Black woman ran for President. And all of this new information was coming from a White man—a white man with an afro. Before taking this class, I didn't really understand Women's Rights. I didn't really understand politics. I didn't understand the nuances of the Civil Rights Movement. Of course, I knew about Dr. Martin Luther King Jr., but everyone knows about him. Who knew that there were so many Black women at the forefront of the Movement who went largely ignored? Who knew that the Latinos I grew up around in Southern California struggled with race issues? What does it mean to be Chicano? And how is that different from Latino? Aren't they all just really Hispanic? Or, Mexican? And Gay Rights. What? There was a Movement? I grew up with a gay brother so for me Gays always had rights. Tell me more about Stonewall.

My world was opened up to this space—this space that existed for those who were willing to put themselves out there, put themselves out there for a cause. They had a reason. They were on a mission. I was on a mission. I was learning about me. My identity was being formed. I was being shaped as a person, as a feminist.

The essay "Black Men in Public Spaces" taught me that words could be used as a way to question self, self in a world of constant and ever-existing antagonists. Brent Staples was a Black man who was a problem, a problem to the world around him. So was Baldwin. He was Black, gay, ugly and not so sure about God. I too was a problem. I was a young woman who wanted more from life and from others. As a first-generation college student, I wanted a world that was foreign to me. I wanted an education, independence and power. Dr. Wilson introduced me to all of this.

I remember my fourth-grade teacher's comments on my report card. He wrote, "Tammy is refined." Several years after high school, I ran into the father of a close friend of mine at a restaurant where I was waiting tables to put myself through college. After reacquainting ourselves and sharing fond memories, Mr. Tolchin said to me: "You know, you have always been different from the other girls. They were all so silly and you were always so mature and focused." Mature? Focused? I never really thought of myself as focused. All the other girls had gone off to schools like Oberlin, University of Southern California and UCLA. They graduated in four years, and I had just transferred to a state school after a succession of community colleges. None of this seemed to matter, though. My credentials didn't define who I was. I had emerged as this confident, articulate young woman who was able to converse with ease, engage with anyone on any subject, and smile at the end of it at just the right time revealing a beauty and grace that told the world I was in control, and I was... but not with my father.

My father has always made me uneasy. Words that flow so smoothly with others are tentative and clumsy with my dad. I find myself struggling to make meaning; I change my meaning, qualify my meaning and deny my meaning when I am with my father. When my father told me I was no longer a feminist because I was a wife and a mother, I recoiled. I went back to being that little girl in that separate and lonely place with a deep urge to manifest those feelings into language, but I couldn't, and I haven't really been able to since then.

I am not sure if marriage and motherhood are compatible with feminism. And if they are not, then what am I? Am I a bad wife and mother or just a bad feminist? Maybe I am neither. Feminism to me is a word, a part of the language of our culture. But, like all words, feminism is merely an expression of our feelings. Feminism isn't a title you can put on and take off. Feminism is the feeling you get when you know that thing between your legs doesn't define you. Feminism is a deep-rooted understanding that you are more than your outward appearance. Feminism is a full expression of who you are, beyond the roles and the labels. Feminism comes from within; it's not a title you can claim or attach to someone else. Feminism is personal. Feminism is a journey of the soul.

A feminist is not male or female. A feminist is a woman who can walk into a boardroom full of men and command a presence at the table. And, a feminist is a man who is willing to relinquish his privilege long enough to welcome her—and her insight. A feminist is not bound by defined gender roles and expectations. A feminist is my fourth-grade teacher, Mr. Angeles. He opened the eyes of a nine-year-old girl to the endless possibilities waiting out there by sharing his stories of growing up in Hawaii and expecting nothing but the best from her. A feminist is Mr. Tolchin. Along with opening my eyes to the parts of me I could not see, he raised a feminist daughter who is a successful immigration attorney and activist. And then there's Dr. Wilson. Dr. Wilson broke the silence. Dr. Wilson gave me words. He gave me language. He gave me power.

A feminist is you, daddy. You taught me to change my tire so I wouldn't need to flag down a man. You called me "Tommy" when you needed help because you understand the androgyny that exists in each of us. You indulged my verbal challenges because you knew I could go toe to toe with the intellectual capacity of any man. And most importantly, before I became a wife and a mother, you once said to me, "You will get married, but you won't stay married." You said this because you know the institution of marriage is limited. It is limited and constrained within the context of outdated and antiquated ideals. You said this because you knew I was and still am bigger than these ideals. You said this because you saw feminism in me. You were projecting, daddy.

What you saw in me was also in you. You were wrong, daddy. I am a feminist, and so are you.

in retrospect
~circa 2023

In 2005 I began writing the essay "Why I am a Feminist."

I was six months pregnant with my second child taking a post graduate course in creative non-fiction, when I reflected on the meaning of feminism after being married for four years and becoming a mother. I came back to this essay and completed it by 2009 after the birth of my daughter, my third and last child. The essay interrogates my experiences as a young woman and the influences on me as I began to develop my feminist voice. As I look at this essay today, I am struck by the absence of women. I talk about my relationship with my father and his presence in my life and how the lessons I learned helped to shape my views about gender roles and expectations. I also include influential male teachers. While my father and male teachers had a positive influence on me, it is an overstatement to suggest they are the reason I am, indeed, a feminist. Both my editor and a friend who was kind enough to provide me content level feedback noted the all-male cast in my piece. I sat with this critique for some time trying to make sense of this contradiction—a collection of essays about my experiences as a mother, wife and feminist that highlight the influences of men.

In the fourteen years since I completed that essay, I have gone through two seven-year cycles of life and transformation. In my early thirties, I was trying to fit into a prescribed role. I had a beautiful home, a husband, three children and a career. Although I vocalized my feminist point of view at every opportunity, deep inside I didn't feel independent; I didn't feel free. I felt bound; I felt obligated; I felt the walls closing in. These feelings are documented in a journal I had been keeping since 1999.

It is an interesting life that I live now. It is a life of monotony. I have a new baby, a toddler and a husband. Can all of these things be compatible with feminism? This is how I have identified myself. Now many of the lines that I have drawn have been blurred. How do I reconcile having a sexist husband with being a feminist? It seems that his sexism affects the way I live my life. His adhering to traditional gender roles inhibits my ability to be fully who I want to be...I imagined a life of world travel, enriching studies, activism and the entertainment of dates at my whim. I keep wondering: How did I get here? A wild feminist in graduate school, has now become a wife and a mother sporting sensible shoes and khakis from Eddie Bauer. -**February 2, 2005**

A year after completing that essay, I started writing other essays that are now a part of this book. That inquiry into the meaning of feminism and the other labels I had attached to myself opened the door to all of the other inquiries and interrogations that enabled me to walk away from my home and my marriage. The questions I raised about the contradictions in marriage, motherhood and feminism were real for me then and even more real for me now, fourteen years later. Those questions were rooted in my childhood memories of my own family, my parents and the roles they played on the stage that was my home. The clearly defined gender roles crept into my marriage despite my best efforts to abate them.

Everything I have ever studied in psychology and all of the insight I gained from years in therapy suggests who we marry and what our marriages look like are a reflection of the relationships we witnessed and experienced in our childhoods, and I am here to testify to this truth.

I had one of the few two parent households in my friend group while growing up. My parents were always physically present. They were there when I returned from school and always around on the weekends. Both my parents were cooks, so I always had homecooked hot meals. My father retired from the military when I was in kindergarten. His service earned him a pension and good health insurance, providing me a sense of financial security and stability. We always had the things we needed. This was my perception. I am well aware as a parent now there are things that go on behind the scenes that make the magic on stage happen—things children may never know or understand. But, from my point of view, we were a middle-class family. Middle-class for me meant there were two parents and a house and the utilities didn't get shut off and the rent was paid.

My father was the bread winner, and my mother was the homemaker. They had very clear roles. They seemed to enjoy their roles, and they played them well. Our home was open to anyone. There were always people present. Our friends, family, extended family, distant cousins and play cousins. My parents entertained often, especially on holidays. My mother was known for her cooking and my father his baking. Our house was always a stop on the holiday route. My parents were generous people; they still are. My mother has a kindness and a selflessness that permeated everything she did. This was especially true when it came to my father. I witnessed a woman who sacrificed her time, energy, desires and dreams for a marriage, a man, a family. For many, this is what is means to be a good wife and a good mother. I am not sure which of these was most important or her number one priority, but, from my vantage point, my father always came first. As a girl child, I felt insignificant. I have even felt this way as an adult woman, as a mother and as a wife needing her mother. I longed for my mother to choose me. I wanted to be the most important person in her world. I wanted affirmation. I wanted her to see me. As a woman, I wanted her to hear me. I needed empathy from her as I trudged through the challenges I experienced in my marriage. There was constant conflict rooted in the power dynamics between my husband and me. I wanted my voice to be heard and valued. I was educated; I had a career and my own bank account. He didn't *hear me or see me.* I wonder if my father saw my mother—not the role, the person. The woman behind the innumerable selfless acts. Writing this feels like betrayal; I am betraying my mother. And it feels liberating; I am freeing myself.

A year after I moved out of my marital home, I was telling a friend about my desire to get back into theater and take some classes. He said he didn't know I was into theater, and he just knew me as "Ron's wife." I knew that my marriage had become intolerable. That is the reason I left. But, to be known only as someone's wife and not a person with human desires and hopes and dreams was devastating. I was insignificant. The person behind the role was invisible. Ron and Tammy had become a pair. We became one. That one was mostly him. I found myself deferring to him even as I rebelled against his controlling nature and narcissism. Each time I deferred, I lost more of myself. I sacrificed my sense of self to be in a marriage with him. His voice was the resounding voice in our home. It was literally louder, always louder, and it held all of the authority. At that time, it seemed easier to defer than to demand. I was trying to protect my kids from the conflicts, and I was trying to protect myself from the humiliation. The arguments always left me feeling humiliated and diminished. His tone was harsh and condescending. His words were biting. Much like my father's.

In the essay "Why I am a Feminist", I write about my ability to use language and words. But this advantage in other spaces with other people was absent with my father. I don't delve into the disconnect in that piece. Fourteen years ago, I didn't have the capacity to do this. I was deeply entrenched in the marriage that had chipped away at my sense of self. I couldn't see clearly. I was emulating what I saw in my childhood. I was selflessly trying to maintain a marriage and hold my family together. In my effort to have some control, I blamed myself for my situation. If I created it, then I could change it. That is what I thought. But more damaging was the shame I felt. I was ashamed of myself for being in this relationship. A feminist would not accept this. A feminist would have left this marriage long ago. A feminist would have never married him. So, the question I ask in that essay: "Am I a bad wife and mother or just a bad feminist?" is a valid one. I certainly believed I was a bad feminist. It was, indeed, true when my father told me, "You are not a feminist anymore, Tammy! You're a wife and mother." I had become in some ways my own mother. I was performing the duties. I was playing into the role. The role erased the self, and I was no longer recognizable. I was sad; I was tired; I was angry.

The decision to walk away from my marriage is one of the most important decisions I have made in my life. My marriage was informed by the uneasiness I felt growing up when talking to my father and the disappointment I had in my mother for not being more emotionally present. The choice I made in a husband was a reflection of what I felt as a child. My husband was harsh and emotionally absent. I felt unseen, misunderstood, deficient. This by no means diminishes the love that my parents gave to me and continue to give to me. How we are able to love is directly connected to how we experienced love as children. They loved to the extent in which they knew how. We all do. My parents have their own stories. So does my ex-husband.

I cannot identify a single feminist woman from my childhood. I understood feminism in theory as a student, then as an activist. I saw men with power, authority and voices. I wanted all of that. When I wrote that essay focused on the power of words and language, I understood that as a tenet of feminism, but the only people I could identify in my life with that kind of power were men. I walked away from my marriage because I was dying inside. My voice was silenced. I walked away from my marriage and my home because I want my children, especially my daughter, to see women who use their voices and fight back.

wind

Wind blowing through the open window

birds chirping

with gratitude to the mother of all

for warm spring like air.

It's different this winter; it's weird; it is.

The winds of change are blowing,

blowing gracefully through the tiny spaces of the

window screen.

a call to the wild
~circa 2021

My first visit to Costa Rica transformed me.

I realized I am more of an introvert than an extrovert. I fell in love with solitude and the peace that comes with nature—the land—the natural world in its rawest, harshest state. In some ways, I fell in love with my deepest, truest self. On my first visit, I interned in a program that afforded me the opportunity to work side-by-side with students from different parts of the world. Each Wednesday and some Saturdays, I put on my *botas*,[3] got on the bus and rode out to the local community and worked on a family farm that was selected to participate in the university's *programa de desarollo la comunitario*.[4] These days were my entrance into the daily lives of real families, real people untethered from the constant pull of commercialization. There were no shopping malls, movie theaters, chain coffee shops or other distractions from the essential connections between family, community and land. By no means am I suggesting that Ticos (the name they call themselves) are disinterested in commercial goods and popular culture and the addicting flavors of McDonald's and KFC. But, by virtue of culture and history and geography, the place maintains a rawness and a connection to the essential. On the farm, I followed the lead of fourth-year students, who had worked for several semesters

---

[3] BOOTS
[4] COMMUNITY DEVELOPMENT PROGRAM

diagnosing the overall efficiency and profitability of the farm and developed a plan to improve the farm's output. These students, through their earlier preparation, coursework in science, and personal development were able to lead projects each week to build chicken coops, build fences, construct biodigesters, plant crops, clear out overgrown areas with machetes, slaughter chickens, and most impressive: walk through these tropical/ jungle areas and identify plants and food and articulate the health benefits and medicinal properties of each plant. Needless to say, I tasted new things but in a much wilder and fresher version. The days in the lowlands of Costa Rica's Limon Province on the Caribbean side of the country were hot and humid, but I soon began to love the feel of the dampness in the air and on my body. It reminded me of all of the things our bodies were created to do and ways in which we adapt to our surroundings.

All of these things drew me into the spirit of the country and *la mujer*—the woman. Doña Lydia[5] *es la mujer.*[6] She was the woman who owned the farm. She watched me every Saturday. She saw me. She knew me. Doña Lydia was a brown woman. She was a wife. She was a mother. She spoke no English, and I spoke only beginning-level Spanish. But we saw each other. We

---

[5] DOÑA IS A TITLE OF RESPECT FOR A MARRIED OR WIDOWED WOMAN.
[6] THE WOMAN

communicated.

Her response to my broken marriage, *"es duro, es dificil, es muy complicado."*[7] She saw me as a woman, like her, even while she saw me participate in the farm duties with the students. I was also a student. I was learning, but what I was learning was different from the students. I was learning about my deep connection to other women. She also saw me as the other—the American. On my first visit to the farm—in the humid lowlands on the Caribbean side of Costa Rica—I wore khaki pants, rubber boots, and a tank top. As a Californian, a sunny day in the open field meant an opportunity to soak in the sun and tan. She knew better. She went inside and brought out a long-sleeved flannel shirt and a sombrero. Using gestures, she told a student to give it to me to put on. I complied. I trust women, but more importantly, I trusted her. She had been working that land for years. She was the farmer. Her husband earned money away from the home. She knew how to use a machete; she watched me closely, so I didn't hurt myself.

One Saturday, she showed me how to kill a chicken. After, she killed it and cleaned it, she put it in a bag for me to take home to my family. I did. I carried the plastic bag with a freshly slaughtered chicken with me on the hour bus ride from the farm back to the

---

[7] HARD, DIFFICULT, VERY COMPLICATED.

university, and I cooked it for dinner that night. Each Saturday morning, I longed for the meals she served us on her crowded patio next to the farm. There were dogs and chickens at our feet, ants and flies abound. But, the food! The food was made in her kitchen by her hands. There was always a beautiful display of beans and rice, sometimes separately, other times together in the famous Costa Rican dish *Gallo Pinto*.[8] Sometimes there was meat, other times a can of tuna was placed on the table. The salads were always fresh and delicious. She made fresh juices—*carambola* or *piña*.[9] Doña Lydia made me feel at home. She created a space for me in her world. This visit left me wanting for more.

I have traveled back three times after that first visit, and it never gets old. Though I did visit a different part of the country—a different climate, different terrain each time. On the fourth visit, I rented a car and drove from the Pacific coast to the Caribbean coast on a nine-day trip. I brought my sister. I needed a witness, someone to see what I had found. I had the same experience with Joshua Tree National Park. My first visit was a rock-climbing trip with a youth group at sixteen years old. I remember the rocks

---

[8] "SPOTTED ROOSTER." COSTA RICA'S NATIONAL DISH OF BEANS AND RICE THAT HAS A SPECKLED APPEARANCE OF BLACK BEANS AGAINST THE WHITE RICE SEASONED WITH THE DELICIOUS CONDIMENT SALSA LIZANO.
[9] STARFRUIT OR PINEAPPLE.

being awe inspiring—both alluring and frightening at the same time. I did not return until almost thirty years later. January of 2020 took me there on a three-day trip with my kids. We drove from the Sonora Desert side on one end to the Mojave Desert on the more popular end with the famous Joshua Tree, which is not really a tree at all, but a tree-like plant that is a part of the Yucca family. The fifty-mile drive was incredible. To witness the beauty that exists in the harshness of the desert and the unforgiving landscape was mesmerizing. I was eager to spot a Big Horn Sheep on our hike to Barker Dam, but no luck. My kids were not as thrilled by it all as I was. I returned again a month later on a day trip and hike with a women's hiking group. Another amazing time to experience the beauty and spirit of the desert. This inspired me to go back, for my birthday in November of 2020, to do a photo shoot for this book. Again, inspired, mesmerized, awed and seduced...the desert called to me in many ways and on many levels.

Big Sur had a similar effect. The landscape/terrain is frightful to say the least, and absolutely sublime to say the most. The contradiction of the place is seductive. The peace was contradicted by the barking seals or sea lions and the crashing waves through the night. The warmth of the sun during the day had no relationship to the frigid air in the night. The roads are tight, yet the view is never-ending, a reminder of the vastness of our planet. It reawakened in me a sense of adventure and courage. Places like Big Sur, Costa Rica and Joshua Tree, are not for those who want to remain comfortable. There is no comfort in wondering what's around that turn on a winding road that can drop you hundreds of feet into the deep ocean. There is no comfort in ninety-degree heat and eighty percent humidity in the lowlands of Costa Rica doing farm labor. There is no comfort in the hot, dry desert. But there is life. There is adventure. And for some of us, there is the self. We find ourselves enraptured in a place. A place that feeds your soul. For me, that place is in the wild.

part five:
mind and body

I am human with human emotions.
I do not have to pretend I am an impregnable force.

I feel a part of myself sheddding like a reptile in the summer. The sensation is liberating, yet confining at the same time. I am moving from one aspect of my life into an unfamliar new life. Fear at this point is my single worst enemy.

Life is how we see ourselves in the mirror.
Are we satisfied with what we see—
our eyes, our lips, our hair, our teeth our bodies?
This shapes our life in many ways.
The mirror is our mind.

Life is. Nothing can change that.
What can change, however, is how I respond to life.
Will I be flexible and bend with the road or will I stand stiff as a board and break?
The road is never straight.
The bend appears when you least expect it.

I feel like something is happening...
I feel much more free;
free to live life—
life according to me.

All I know is I am beginning to enjoy myself as me.
All of me. The good and the bad.

an afterword

In several parts of this book,

I refer to going into my seventh cycle of seven years. Quite literally that means I am approaching forty-nine years of age. In an abstract sense, the seven-year cycle is a concept accepted by some in the fields of psychology, particularly in human development, and astrology and to a much narrower degree, science. For me, this concept represents life changes and shifts on an emotional and spiritual level. Much of what I have seen in my life makes logical sense on a human development level. But, from a deeper perspective relative to my spiritual growth and self-actualization, all of the experiences I have shared in this book, directly or indirectly, are related to the place in which I find myself now—entering my seventh cycle of seven years. The sum total of my life experiences—the joy, the pain, the trauma and the challenges—are why I am able to write this book. They are why I am able to tell my story. This cycle in my life is a reflection of an enlightenment of sorts or a spiritual awakening. As I tracked major life experiences at each seven-year period, I noticed transition and shifting in my thinking and perspective. Each period builds upon the one before it and informs the period that follows.

In the essay "Feminism is a Trauma Response," I reveal that I experienced sexual trauma from seven years old until I was fourteen. At seven, we begin to learn how authority works. We see the adults in our lives as people with power over us. If that power is misused, we can become mentally and emotionally stifled in our development. I have only recently been able to overcome the hang ups I have around my sexuality and my body. I spent most of my life in shame and deference to male partners. The loss of agency and absence of boundaries and healthy authority shaped my view of myself, my body and how I enter into relationships with men. The cycles that follow the sexual abuse reveal patterns of internal and external conflicts around power and control. Around fourteen, we begin to question our own identity and are challenged by external influences.

As a survivor of sexual abuse, I began seeking solace in religion. Fundamentalist Christianity found me at sixteen years old—the precise time I needed to be forgiven for my "dirty little secret." Our emotional and sexual development also begins at this time. Through the church and baptism and accepting Jesus into my heart as my personal savior, I was forgiven. But, the tenets of fundamentalist Christianity around sexuality tortured my adolescent mind and spirit. I found myself harboring guilt about every impure thought and desire. This exacerbated the shame I already felt about not speaking out against the abuse as a child. I am dirty; sexuality is dirty; desire is dirty.

Around twenty-one years old, the time in which we legally become an adult in all areas of our lives, many of us become aligned with our passions. By twenty, I had left the church, found feminism in the college classroom, had my first abortion and began therapy to deal with my childhood trauma. Around twenty-eight, I married, had my first child and earned my second college degree. I was on track to the ideal life: wife, mother and career woman. A few years later, I bought a four-bedroom house with granite counter tops, stainless steel appliances and spent hours watching HGTV and the Food Network. We entertained often, and we looked good doing it. I had it all according to cultural standards and expectations.

At thirty-five years old, the time in which many of us begin stepping into our own authority, I had become disillusioned with marriage. It was exhausting preparing canapes and stuffed mushrooms and homemade cupcakes with real vanilla beans. I had given birth to three children and adrenal fatigue had taken over my body. Around this time, I also started writing this book. A year later, I moved out of my marital home and started on a solo journey to find me. I took my first sabbatical as a college professor at forty-one, an internship in urban agriculture on the Caribbean side of Costa Rica. This trip changed me; it re-awakened the passion I had in my early twenties. The geospatial reality of Costa Rica reconnected me to the deepest part of my soul—my essence, inducing another shift. The work on the land, literally and figuratively, grounded me. All that I had acquired in my forty-one years of life meant nothing compared to that return to the self, a Sankofa[1] of sorts. The essence of my soul's desire had nothing, at all, to do with being a mother or wife or feminist or college professor. These were all just experiences meant to help me find and reconnect to that essence.

A year later, at forty-two, I accepted a faculty position in California and returned to my birth place. The sixth cycle is a time of personal reinvention and discarding of stereotypes and believing in ourselves. In the essay "la regresión," I discuss the challenges I faced coming home and the lessons I learned. I experienced the tragic death of two brothers; I lived through crisis with all three of my children; I officially divorced, and I finished writing this book. This very dark period has prepared me for a spiritual awakening. Our seventh cycle of seven years is about authenticity and truth, clarity of purpose and self-acceptance. I am in the process of letting go of the roles and

---

[1] SANKOFA IS AN AFRICAN WORD FROM THE AKAN TRIBE IN GHANA. THE LITERAL TRANSLATION IS "IT IS NOT TABOO TO FETCH WHAT IS AT RISK OF BEING LEFT BEHIND."

labels and accepting what is in each moment. The labels wife, mother and feminist no longer have a hold on me. They are not who I am; they are things I do to serve a purpose in a given moment. It is also about the acceptance of others and unconditional love. I am consciously choosing to see others as they are in each moment—to see their humanity. I see all of the experiences and the people I have encountered in my life as gifts, gifts that have offered me the opportunity to expand. I am looking forward to each new seven-year cycle and a new iteration of myself here in this life on this planet.

References

Interview with James Baldwin WFCR Radio Broadcast Collection (MS 741). Special Collections and University Archives. University of Massachusetts Amherst Libraries.

Patricia Hill Collins, "Black Feminist Epistemology," *Black Feminist Thought: Knowledge, Consciousness, and the Politics of Empowerment*, 2nd Edition. New York: Rutledge, Taylor & Francis, 2000.

About the Author

I am a writer, English professor, and mother of three. I spent much of my adult life living on the Southside of Chicago where I learned many lessons and uncovered many truths. I was born and raised in Pasadena, California where I learned to love diversity. On the Southside of Chicago is where I learned to love my Blackness. I have been teaching composition and literature for over twenty years at various colleges. I am currently a tenured faculty member in the Department of English at Moorpark College in Moorpark, California. My greatest wish for my writing students is that they find their truth and learn to trust their voice.